What Nice-o-holics have to say about *Do One Nice Thing*

·····························

"Thanks to you no one has any excuse to just sit there and do nothing."—Liz

"Thank you for giving my family a way to give back! I love teaching my young children that it is so much better to give than to receive, and this is such a neat way to do that. They are all very excited and each making different things to send."—Katrina

"What fun stuff to do! With all the doom and gloom in the world, seeing positive and happy things are good for all of us."—Margaret

"Your work matters a great deal. I share the e-mails with my graduate students and colleagues. The messages are always one *very* bright spot in a daily sea of business and news e-mails. Your e-mails encourage me to 'make a difference.'"—Steve

"I just wanted to tell you how much I love *Do One Nice Thing*. It really brightens my day. I've made a resolution to have more positive things in my life, and I found your website just in time."—Jenny

"I am a huge fan. The ideas are so easy and inexpensive. There is no reason not to do a nice thing! I love that by ten on Mondays I have often already done a good thing. What a great way to start the week."—Francesca

"Your efforts have had a wonderful ripple effect around the world. Around the world! Can you even fathom that?" —Kim

Do One Nice Thing

Little Things You Can Do to Make the World a Lot Nicer

Debbie Tenzer

Crown Publishers
NEW YORK

Copyright © 2009 by Debra Gross Tenzer

All rights reserved.
Published in the United States by Crown Publishers,
an imprint of the Crown Publishing Group,
a division of Random House, Inc., New York.
www.crownpublishing.com

CROWN and the Crown colophon are registered trademarks
of Random House, Inc.

Portions of this work originally appeared on the website
www.doonenicething.com.

Library of Congress Cataloging-in-Publication Data

Debbie Tenzer
Do one nice thing / Debbie Tenzer.—1st ed.
1. Kindness. 2. Helping behavior. 3. Interpersonal
relations. I. Title
BJ1533.K5T46   2009
177'.7—dc22   2008050631

ISBN 978-0-307-45380-8

Printed in the United States of America

The Do One Nice Thing logo was designed by
John Michael Pugsley.

This book is printed on Norbrite recycled paper.

Design by Cindy LaBreacht

10 9 8.7 6 5 4 3 2 1

First Edition

Dedication

Sometimes in life there's a glorious moment when all the disparate strands of experience, struggle, and dreaming come together. Suddenly it's clear that everything you've ever done was meant to happen. All the puzzle pieces have finally fallen into place, and now, miraculously, *your entire life makes sense!*

This is not that moment.

I never thought that someone would ask me to write a book, or that I'd create a website, or correspond with thousands of people all over the globe.

I never imagined that Girl Scouts in South Carolina would ask me how to send crayons to a school in Kentucky; or that church youth-group members in Alabama would ask me how to help homeless people in Michigan. I never thought that a rabbi in California would ask me how to mail toys to children in Afghanistan. And I certainly never imagined that I would know what to tell them.

I never could have conceived that soldiers would send photos to me of smiling children in war zones, clutching notebooks, blankets, and teddy bears that they received from Americans. Or that in gratitude the soldiers would send me the flag that flew over their base.

Most of all, I never dreamed that countless kind people around the world would share their stories and ideas with me and participate in a kindness project each week. I don't know how I got here, and I don't think about it much. But I know I wouldn't be writing these words if not for all those nice people, Do One Nice Things' "Nice-o-holics," and I'm tremendously grateful to them.

So even though my name is on the cover, this is their book.

Remember, people will judge you
by your *actions*, not your intentions.
You may have a heart of gold—
but so does a hard-boiled egg.

—Anonymous

Contents

*These projects are easy for children to do.

2

Do One Nice Thing for Children

3

Do One Nice Thing for Pets and the Planet

Contents

4

Do One Nice Thing That Heals **91**

Contents

5

Do One Nice Thing in Town **125**

Contents

6

7

8
Just Click! Do One Nice Thing Online 221

Welcome

Have you ever had one of those days when you wish you could turn down the volume on *everything*? Welcome to Monday, my toughest day of the week.

So not surprisingly, on a Monday I was having lunch with a few girlfriends when the conversation turned sour. My friends bemoaned the Iraq war, terrorism, global warming, hunger, crime, and on and on. I thought, "Gee, if I wanted to get depressed, I could've stayed home and watched the news." Anxiety is contagious. And as I listened to my friends' anger rising, my head began to pound. Like a turtle, I quietly retreated into my shell.

Driving home I had a little talk with myself: "Hey! Lose the loser attitude. Yes, we face huge problems in the world, and no, I don't have the faintest idea how to solve them. But even if I can't do much, I'm positive *I can do something.*"

And it hit me:

→ I can't end hunger, but I *can* donate cans to a food bank.

→ I can't fix needy schools, but I *can* give them my kids' old books.

→ I can't end the war, but I *can* send a phone card so a soldier can be comforted by calling home.

I realized that helping does not have to be difficult, expensive, or time-consuming. It starts by doing just *one* nice thing. At that moment, I committed to doing at least one nice thing for someone one day every week. By setting the bar at that realistic height, I felt this was a promise I could keep. I chose Monday, my hardest day, because I'm always tired and cranky. I reasoned that if I could make Mondays better, maybe the rest of the week would go more smoothly.

Feeling empowered, I began *nicing* regularly: I gave away old clothes . . . brought a cup of hot coffee to the school crossing guard . . . left a snack in my mailbox for my mail carrier—I was rolling now! My

Debbie Tenzer

Mondays began to improve. I made a list of ideas of easy-to-do nice things, and e-mailed it to sixty of my friends, inviting them to join me on Do One Nice Thing Mondays.

Good news traveled fast. My friends told their friends, and their friends told *their* friends, and all of them wanted to help. My idea evolved into a website, www.DoOneNiceThing.com. It now attracts millions of people in more than eighty countries. I never expected anything like this.

One Nice Thing Every Monday

The Do One Nice Thing website embraces good people everywhere—people of all faiths, backgrounds, and opinions. We don't agree on everything—we don't have to. We are united by our desire to help others.

Each Monday I post a nice thing for the week, and people participate all over the world in various ways. Many people do our nice thing of the week—for example, send pencils to a needy school in Kentucky. But maybe they'd rather bring pencils to a local school or cookies to co-workers. Great! Any way a person wants to help is wonderful. The more deliberate kindness we can create in the world, the better.

Ideas are often sent to me by Do One Nice Thing

Do One Nice Thing

members, whom I call Nice-o-holics because once you do a few nice things, *you get hooked.* This book is about our favorite nice things and some of the marvelous people who do them.

Who are *Do One Nice Thing*'s Nice People? They're people who teach needy children and coach their athletic teams; they bike, run, and skydive to raise money for medical research and affordable housing; they volunteer in homeless shelters and help underprivileged students apply to college. They are the people who buy goats that sustain Rwandan villages and send packages to U.S. service members in harm's way.

Other Nice People hand out cookies to strangers, bring hot soup to sick friends, and give hugs when we need them most. A wall in my office is covered with Nice-o-holics' pictures. When I look at the faces—different ages, colors, and nationalities—I remember how much goodness we are all capable of feeling and expressing.

I think there's a real benefit to doing a nice thing every week. It's like strength training for the soul. With all the bad news in the world, crisis after crisis pounding us, it's easy to become numb. By making kindness a habit and helping on a regular basis, we can keep our compassion muscles strong.

I am continually amazed by one fact: One person's small acts can lead to big results.

Debbie Tenzer

Nice-o-holics have . . .

➜ mailed more than 140,000 pounds of school supplies to U.S. soldiers in Afghanistan, who give
them to local children so they can study

➜ sent countless books to schools, libraries, and
hospitals

➜ contributed numerous backpacks to foster children, who often carry the little they own from
home to home in garbage bags

➜ donated thousands of blankets to U.S. soldiers in
Iraq, who gave them to local people living without electricity or heat

➜ delivered tens of thousands of cans of food, packages of pasta, and frozen turkeys to food banks
at Thanksgiving

How to Use This Book

This book offers more than a hundred ideas. Naturally, I love them all. But I want you to do the nice
things that will be the most meaningful to you. Here
are some suggestions:

A good way to start is to scan the Contents pages
and see which ideas grab your attention: helping
children, writing to soldiers, comforting sick people,

Do One Nice Thing

protecting the planet, doing nice things with your friends, helping in your town or in the larger global community. Does one category touch your heart more than the others? If so, that's where to start.

If you like to plan in advance, pick a chapter as your monthly theme—for example, "Do One Nice Thing for Children." Then decide how you will help children each week by selecting ideas from that chapter.

Maybe you prefer to choose randomly. Close your eyes, flip through the book, and stop on any page to discover your week's nice thing.

Kids can do lots of nice things! There are loads of wonderful projects that children can do at school, at home, in clubs, and in their houses of worship. Projects that are especially fun and easy for kids to do are marked with an asterisk in the Contents so you—and they—can find them effortlessly.

Do you have a birthday or a get-together coming up? Find ideas in the chapter "Do One Nice Thing with Friends and Family" for ways to do a good deed with the people you love while also celebrating.

Decide on a weekly project with members of your family, house of worship, club, or office. You can also do one nice thing with the people you care about, regardless of where they live. Your weekly nice thing can connect you no matter how many miles or continents separate you.

Debbie Tenzer

Pressed for time? Do a nice thing in five minutes without even leaving your desk. Scan Chapter 8, "Just Click!" to find out how to do one nice thing online. You can donate free food, mammograms, or children's books; preserve a rain forest; and care for animals just by clicking on a website link.

You can choose a different nice thing every Monday, or do the same thing each week.

Monday is my favorite day to help, but you can pick a different day if you'd like. Any day that ends in *y* is fine. And, of course, you're welcome to do more than one nice thing each week.

Whatever you do, you're going to feel glad you did it. Record the nice things you do in the journal at the back of this book. And when you have an "off" day, which all of us have, when you're feeling frustrated and bugged and nothing is going your way, do one nice thing for yourself. Make yourself a cup of hot tea or chocolate or whatever you like, and take a few quiet moments to read through the journal. By remembering the nice things you've done for others, chances are you'll feel better about yourself.

Getting Our Focus Back

Life has an irritating way of interfering with our intentions. A child or an elderly parent gets sick; an

Do One Nice Thing

emergency occurs at work; a storm slams our city; a loved one in the military is deployed. Or, nothing in particular is going on, but we just get wrapped up in our own lives. Let's face it, sometimes we're nice and sometimes we're not.

We're not bad; we're just not as good as we want to be. Amid all the hustle and noise, we lose our focus. Unfortunately, there are lots of distractions out there. But we can deal with them and whatever else life throws at us. We can harness the tremendous power in our hearts, together. We can refocus on what matters: making the world better. That is what this book is about.

I'm not going to preach to you about how to live your life. I'm no angel. I'm as self-centered and impatient as everyone else, and I don't have any especially deep insights. But I do know this: Right now we are standing between a past that we can't change, and a future that is as limitless as our imaginations. We *can* make the world better.

Maybe we don't know how to solve The Big Problems . . . yet. But in the meantime we can hit a bull's-eye for fifty-two smaller problems each year, and that feels pretty darn good. Find your mark, take aim, and join us. Here we go.

Debbie Tenzer

Note: Some "nice things" fit into more than one category, so I used my best judgment to select the chapter that seemed like the best fit.

Also, the details in this book about websites and organizations were accurate when the book went to press. Changes will inevitably occur, however, so please visit www.DoOneNiceThing.com for updated addresses and information.

Do One Nice Thing

1

Do One Nice Thing with Friends and Family

It's been said that friends are the people who know all about us and like us anyway. True! But they are so much more. They get our jokes, they've got our backs, and they know what we're thinking even when we don't say a word.

Sometimes all we need from them is a hug, a squirt of laughter, or a reality check. At other times, industrial-strength caring is required—like long phone calls into the night and special deliveries from the Casserole Brigade. And even if we don't hear from them for months or even years, when we need our friends, they come.

So, what do you give those who give so much to you?

This chapter is full of nice things to do with and for your friends—from surprising them with a treat on their desk or doorstep to creating a group charity project or a priceless gift from the heart.

Contrary to what some think, friends are not "a dime a dozen." They are the family we choose—precious and irreplaceable. And if we're really blessed, our family members are also our friends, so this chapter is for them too.

Debbie Tenzer

What's Cooking?

Cook a meal for a friend who recently moved into a new home, is recuperating from an illness, or just needs some love.

Mmmmm. Nothing says love like chicken soup. Its steamy golden goodness always makes us feel better. So when one of my friends needs some TLC after a family-rocking event, I head straight for the kitchen, pull out my big soup pot, and get busy.

Here is my favorite chicken soup recipe, given to me by my dear friend Ziva, which I now give to you. It is so easy that even I can't spoil it. I'm not sure that it will cure what ails you, but it will definitely warm some hearts.

Ziva's Chicken Soup

You will need these ingredients:
6 chicken legs or thighs
2 peeled onions, whole
1 peeled parsnip, whole
6 celery stalks, chopped into 1-inch pieces
6 carrots, peeled and chopped into 1-inch
   pieces

Do One Nice Thing

1 bunch of flat-leaf parsley, whole

1 bunch of fresh dill, whole

1 bay leaf

1 tablespoon salt

1 teaspoon pepper

1 chicken bouillon cube

Toss everything into a big pot. (I told you it was easy.) Cover with 10 quarts of cold water and heat. Bring to a boil; then simmer for an hour. Discard the onions, parsnip, parsley, and dill. Strain the carrots, celery, and chicken; store in a covered container in the refrigerator. Cool the broth and store it, covered, overnight in the refrigerator. Skim off the fat. When cool, cut up the chicken. Then return the carrots, celery, and cut-up chicken to the broth in a big pot. You may also add other vegetables, noodles, rice, or dumplings. Heat thoroughly and adjust the seasoning.

•••••••••••••••••••••••••

"We had just moved into our new house when I came down with the flu. My two toddlers had it too. When my husband arrived home from work he was greeted by our next-door neighbor, a widow in her seventies. He mentioned that we were sick. An hour later she knocked at the door carrying a pot of homemade potato soup, just like my mom used to make. What a healing effect that had—on the tummy and on the soul!"—Sharon

Debbie Tenzer

Hooked on Running

**Run or walk with your friends
in a charity marathon.
Or if you'd prefer to exercise
your administrative muscles,
how about assisting the staff?**

Sharlene Wills is a devout distance runner. She trains regularly, competes in marathons, and enjoys training off the beaten path in the hills. She also happens to be blind.

She said, "I couldn't pursue this wonderful sport without the unselfish and voluntary help of many very nice people." She often runs with a runners' organization called LA Leggers. Some of the Leggers members volunteer to be tethered to her in order to guide her during her runs.

Sharlene explained, "One of the volunteers, Maneesha Bhate, is a pretty fast runner, having finished the L.A. Marathon in about four hours. She's very unselfish, though, and often paces or runs with slower folks like me, even when they don't have to be guided."

• • • • • • • • • • • • • • • • • • •

"Technically, I participated in the AIDS Run, but I'm not sure if what I did qualifies as running; maybe it

Do One Nice Thing

was the AIDS Waddle. It may be a cliché to say it was one of the hardest things I have ever done, but also one of the most satisfying, but it's true. I developed a family unit with the group of strangers from a variety of backgrounds that I trained with. We all supported each other over a five-month training period and then we ran the marathon together. When I was dragging, someone was there to encourage me to complete it. And the great thing was we did it to raise money for a wonderful cause."—Mike

Debbie Tenzer

The Potluck Club

Get together with your friends for a potluck meal and moral support—then select a charitable cause to support together.

"My friends and I get together periodically at my house to make greeting cards for the troops. It's a lot of fun and we have a great time 'solving *all* the world's problems.' Instead of bringing me hostess gifts (who needs more stuff?), I suggested we start a donation piggy bank. Whenever we get together, Matilda the Pig gets fed with whatever anybody wants to give.

"Last Christmas was Matilda's first full year of 'feedings,' and with the proceeds I was able to buy holiday gifts for a needy family and send five care packages to the troops in Iraq and Afghanistan."—Gisela

Do One Nice Thing

PARTY!

For your next birthday or anniversary, ask your friends to bring you a gift that you can donate to a local school or shelter, such as art supplies or canned goods.

"For my thirtieth birthday last fall, I had a huge party with all of my friends and relatives. But I didn't really need anything, and I didn't want more unusable items to clutter up my home. So instead, I asked all of my party guests to bring one item of nonperishable food, which would be donated to my local food bank. The response was overwhelming! The party was held in the basement of my church, so we just had to take the contributions upstairs to where we always collect food for the food bank. It took four trips to carry it all."—Laura

Debbie Tenzer

The Gift That Keeps on Giving

What should you buy for a friend who has everything? Nothing! Send a card and mail a donation to charity.

You can also give when you shop on eBay. EBay Giving Works offers thousands of auctions that donate to charities. When you shop, look for the charity ribbons or search for charities. If you're a seller, list items to benefit a cause that you care about (www.eBayGivingWorks.com).

••••••••••••••••••••••••

"I do online banking and pay my bills with automatic billing. So I designated our local food pantry to receive $5.00 per week. It's money they need, and I won't miss it because it's already in my budget."—Susan

Do One Nice Thing

BINGO!

**Invite friends over to play a game
and chat instead of going out.**

My girlfriends and I get together every so often to eat lunch at one of our homes and play mah-jongg, also known as mahj. I confess: I am a terrible player. How bad am I? My friends need to refresh my memory about the rules every time we play. They also guide me throughout the game and grant me "takeovers" when I make a really bad mistake. This is mercy mahj.

But it doesn't matter because I don't come for the game—I come for the company. I love seeing Judi, Gail, and Joanne. We don't have the chance to hang out together as much as we used to, so we make the most of our mahj games. While we munch on our lunch, we share work and family news, skewer politicians, and swap tips on everything from acupuncture to jury duty. And sometimes I even get lucky and win a round of mahj.

. . . .

"The other night, instead of going to a movie and spending the money on tickets, an activity where no conversation happens, we used the money to buy a

Debbie Tenzer

board game. We had a great time playing and invited friends over to play. The next time we're tempted to see a movie, we have a couple of new games to play with our friends. When we get tired of the games, we'll give them to a charity so kids can use them."
—Melanie

Do One Nice Thing

Highly Recommended

Write a "letter of recommendation" for one of your friends, or add it to a birthday card. Mention all of her or his best qualities and why she/he is precious to you. I guarantee you are going to make someone happy.

A friend of mine always dreamed of finishing college but he was unable to pursue his studies because he needed to work. After many years, he was finally able to return to school.

I was flattered when he asked me to write a recommendation for him, and when he read it, he was very touched. His reaction made me realize that he didn't know how much I appreciated him. How often do we take the time to tell our friends these things?

Debbie Tenzer

Too Big to Wrap

Give your loved ones a one-of-a-kind gift: time with you.

Give the people you love hand-made coupons offering to:

➜ make them breakfast in bed

➜ keep them company on a trip to the doctor, DMV, or mall

➜ help them clean out their closets or garage

➜ work with them in their garden

➜ take them out for a movie, concert, dinner, or hike

My children used to make coupons for each other as birthday gifts. When they were small the coupons said: "I will read you a story" . . . "I will play a game with you" . . . "I will bring you cookies." And when they were older: "I will make your breakfast" . . . "I will clean your room" . . . "I will give you piggyback rides all day."

These gifts cost nothing, but their value? *Priceless.*

• • • • • • • • • • • • • • • • •

"My husband brings me breakfast in bed on Sunday mornings."—Cynthia

Do One Nice Thing

Card Shower

Shower someone with love and good wishes: Organize a "thinking of you" or birthday card shower. Ask all of his or her friends and family members to participate by sending cards on a specific day. What a sweet surprise!

"We have a friend who was paralyzed in a car accident last summer. As his birthday approached in February, we sent out self-addressed stamped cards to all of our friends and family asking them to help us overload his mailbox on his birthday. He received over one hundred cards and made some new friends."—Mary

Debbie Tenzer

Pass It On

Remember that especially comforting, inspiring, or touching thing someone said to you? Say it to someone else. Who knows? You might start a positive chain reaction.

Here are some things people have said to me. Now consider them yours.

••••••••••••••••••••••

"Just hearing your voice makes me happy."
"You have no idea how much you helped me."
"You inspire me."
"What you did took courage."
"I feel so good whenever I see you."

••••••••••••••••••••••

Use this space to write down heartfelt things that people have said or written to you.

Do One Nice Thing

Secret Admirer

**Put a flower on a co-worker's desk
or friend's doorstep.**

"Yesterday it was cold and gloomy. I bought a bunch of daffodils for each of my staff to brighten the day. Whenever you look at daffodils, it just makes you smile."—La Donna

• •

"I have had a great time with my office; I've discovered a website where you can order flowers and have them delivered from the closest florist. So far, I've sent them to most of the office, with no one the wiser about who's sending them. It's worked quite well, and brought a lot of joy and mystery to the office."—Joi

Debbie Tenzer

Give 'Em Some Sugar

Secretly place candies on the desks of the people you work with or on the pillows of the people you love.

For a week I carried a bag of chocolate Hershey's Kisses in my purse and handed them out as I went about my business:

→ I left one shiny foil-wrapped kiss on the sign-in sheet at my doctor's office.

→ I pressed a couple more into the hand of the young woman who bagged my groceries.

→ When I made a deposit at my bank, I slipped one to the teller.

Everyone was delighted! I'm not sure what made people happier—chocolate itself or the surprise of receiving some.

This nice habit was making me a little *too happy*, however. Every time I gave away a candy, I gave one to myself too. So now I keep just a few in my purse, and I give all of them away. (Well, most of them.)

Do One Nice Thing

"Since my son was about fifteen, on Valentine's Day he has gotten up early and anonymously delivered a flower and a small box of chocolates to the doorstep of the girls he knows who don't have boyfriends. I'm sure the girls have a much better day for having someone think of them on such a romantic day."—Dawn

Debbie Tenzer

Ba-da BING!

Make someone laugh. Jokes are available on www.AhaJokes.com, and many other websites, or visit www.YouTube.com for great videos of laughing babies.

We should laugh more. There's nothing like a great big chuckle, chortle, or guffaw to energize us and lighten our day. Some researchers believe that when we laugh, feel-good hormones are released in our bodies, reducing stress and spreading protective antibodies inside of us. So not only does laughing make us feel happy but it literally makes us feel better.

When I was writing this chapter, I suddenly found myself needing an infusion of laughter. I accidentally injured my shoulder and it was painfully not funny. I quickly grew tired of people asking me, "How did you do it?" and was equally tired of explaining.

Then I had an idea. I asked Do One Nice Thing members to guess how I did it and make me laugh. Boy, did they deliver. Here are some of their ideas of how I might have injured my shoulder, and my thoughts:

➜ arm wrestling for the last piece of chocolate cake
(Yes, that could be me.)

Do One Nice Thing

29

→ herding caribou *(Not in this lifetime.)*

→ boxing *(What? And hurt my face?)*

→ painting a fresco on my office ceiling *(Those stick figures look really good up there.)*

→ whipping my hat through the air while bull riding *(I admit to having a cowgirl fantasy, but that's not it.)*

→ twisting into a pretzel to impress a handsome yoga teacher *(Nobody is that handsome.)*

→ swinging on the trapeze at the circus *(Do I get to wear a tutu?)*

→ crashing onto the ice when my partner dropped me during our ice-dancing routine *(He's toast.)*

→ and finally . . . bending over backward to help people *(Yay!)*

So how did I *really* injure my shoulder? All I can say is, I'll *never* pitch for the Los Angeles Dodgers again.

Of course, there's always that trapeze job. . . .

Debbie Tenzer

Scrappy Together

Invite your friends over to make a scrapbook for a special friend or beloved teacher. Each person can create a page or contribute a photo or story. Then put them all together for a gift that will be treasured.

"Mrs. K. is a legend at our school. She has taught kindergarten there for twenty-five years, and getting into her class makes you feel special. She is an incredible person—patient, fair, and so loving with each and every child. My oldest son blossomed in her class.

"I knew early on that my son's kindergarten year was going to be one that he would never forget, and I wanted both him and his teacher to remember it in a visual way. From the beginning of the year, I knew I wanted to make a scrapbook for her.

"In the book, I included photos of all the field trips, vivid art projects, candid snapshots, special events, and a photo portrait of every student. I had also collected two quotes from each child. One quote was, 'I love Mrs. K because . . .' The other was, 'What I love most about kindergarten is . . .' On the last page was a grateful letter from my son and a drawing that

Do One Nice Thing

he had made especially for the book. I also included a letter from me, thanking her for being so wonderful.

"One morning during the last week of school, my son and I went into her class extra early and presented the gift to her. She was overwhelmed. She said in all her years of teaching, no one had ever given her such a beautiful gift. She showed it to the principal, every teacher, and all her friends. To this day whenever I see her with a friend outside of school, she introduces me as 'the one who made the scrapbook for me.'"—Susan

Debbie Tenzer

2
Do One Nice Thing for Children

There's an old expression: "Insanity is hereditary. You get it from your kids."

Well, then inspiration must be hereditary also. To give you an idea of how much children can inspire us, consider this:

→ Keegan, age seven, participated in a 5K multiple sclerosis walk to honor his aunt who has the disease.

→ Allie, ten, organized a fund-raiser for the Detroit Zoo.

→ Josh, thirteen, led a charity walk to raise money for a food bank. He enlisted his grandparents to walk too.

→ Megan, eleven, created a "card ministry." Assisted by her little sister Ally, nine, Mom, and Grandma, she makes greeting cards and gift baskets for senior citizens.

→ Tatiana, eight, received an award sticker every year at school. When she noticed that another little girl worked hard but did not receive an award, Tatiana gave hers to the other child.

In this chapter you'll find all kinds of ideas to help children in need, from foster kids in California to orphans in Africa. It will also help you teach the lucky children in your life how to make the world better. Or, then again, maybe they'll teach you.

Blue Roofs
in Mississippi

Donate something to a school.
Inquiring minds need it.

Eden Elementary School, located in the Appalachian Mountains, never has enough school supplies. Send any of the following: pencils, paper (notebooks or loose leaf), glue sticks, scissors, crayons, erasers, markers, folders, backpacks. Mail to: Eden Elementary Family Resource Center, Route 645 Eden Lane, Inez, KY 41224.

You can also help by donating funds to Donors Choose (www.DonorsChoose.org), where teachers across the United States post requests online for books, supplies, technology, and more. Then you can select the way you'd like to help.

Following Hurricanes Katrina and Rita, "blue roofs" were what people in the Gulf Coast region called the tarps that covered many homes damaged by the storms.

Jefferson Middle School in Columbia, Mississippi, had been lucky. Spared the devastation that others experienced, the school was still standing and became an anchor in the storm. It opened its doors and

Do One Nice Thing

hearts to hundreds of students whose schools and homes had been destroyed. As children arrived from surrounding areas, the size of the student body swelled quickly. Many kids walked into the school with nothing and no one. Overnight JMS teachers and staff became social workers, doctors, and detectives. Heroes. They took care of all the children.

What did these students need? Belts. JMS students wore uniforms and there was a shortage of belts. New students could not afford to buy them. So we dug into our closets and sent belts. We also sent notebooks, binders, paper, and other school supplies. We stayed in touch and continued to send packages.

On the second anniversary of the storm, I called and asked the assistant principal, Angela Burkett, if she needed anything, and she said, "We're doing fine now! We don't need any more help." That was music to my ears. I asked if her students could now do a nice thing for someone else. A bridge in Minnesota had recently collapsed and many children there were hospitalized. Could JMS students make get-well cards for those kids? Yes.

What cards they made! They said, "You can do it, I know you can." "Don't forget God is with you." "I've had a hard time too. Things will get better. Believe me." Out of the mouths and hearts of twelve-year-olds.

Debbie Tenzer

Serving Up Winners

Send new tennis balls to Net Results Junior Tennis, 950 South Cherry Street, Suite 402, Denver, CO 80246 (www.NetResultsOnline.org).

All children are winners. Some just don't know it yet. Net Results Junior Tennis is helping low-income kids in Denver realize their potential and believe in themselves.

Running multiple programs in eight low-performing Denver schools, Net Results gets results. Twice a week after school, the kids get a boost on their academics by receiving specialized attention from trained tutors. However, on non-tutor days the kids get what they really crave: free tennis lessons from professional coaches.

The children learn to set goals, play and work hard, follow rules, and respect coaches and other players. Doing well in high school and going on to college become their goals.

Smashing results: Kids become physically stronger as well as more disciplined, successful, and confident. Although Net Results is not trying to produce the next Wimbledon champ, many of the kids do become strong competitors and participate proudly in tournaments.

Do One Nice Thing

Twelve-year-old Judith joined Net Results after playing with her older brothers, and her coaches say she's *good*. But she doesn't want to play professionally. Her dream is to go to college so she can coach low-income children and teach them what she's learned: "I'm strong. I'm focused. Sometimes I win, and sometimes I lose. But I'm always a winner."

"My goals for tennis this year are being a good sport and to not get mad if I lose!"—Asia, nine

Debbie Tenzer

Nothing Stops a Bullet Like a Ball

Donate used sports equipment and outgrown athletic clothing and shoes to your local recreation center, school, or Big Brothers/ Big Sisters of America in your town (www.bbbs.org).

Darren Erman, a young lawyer from Kentucky, left a top Chicago law firm to be a teacher and assistant basketball coach for two years at an inner-city high school, St. Anthony's in Jersey City, New Jersey.

The school was a safe haven from the neighborhood's pervasive drugs and violence. More than 50 percent of the students' families lived below the poverty line, and crime in the area was rampant. For the school's athletes, basketball was more than a sport: It was a lifeline to a better future.

Darren left his firm, a six-figure salary, and a spacious Chicago apartment and headed east. His next home was a friend's Manhattan apartment, where he slept on an air mattress on the living room floor. Rising at five every morning for his commute to school, he found a passion that had been missing from his life.

Do One Nice Thing

He loved motivating the kids to focus on their future—hopefully one that would be safer and more fulfilling. They needed to get into college, and excellence in basketball would help them. But they would need to perfect their skills off the court too. So in addition to teaching science classes and coaching, Darren took the senior players under his wing, tutored them, and helped them fill out college and scholarship applications.

The team finished 30–0 and was Number Two in the nation. Plus all four of the team's seniors were accepted to college and received scholarships to Division I basketball programs. Was it worth turning his life upside down for? Darren exclaimed, "Definitely!"

Did a teacher, coach, or mentor have a profound impact on your life? Who was it? What lesson did he or she teach that you still embrace today? Can you pass it on to someone else?

For me, that person was Ms. Marilyn Tavares, my dance teacher for many years. She'd challenge me: "Why do what everyone else does? Turn a movement around—or upside down. Don't be afraid." Many years later that insight spurred me to start Do One Nice Thing. Frustrated that I couldn't solve the world's big problems, I turned it upside down and found smaller problems that I could solve. Thank you, Ms. Tavares.

Debbie Tenzer

Make a Wish

**Send toys, books, and other gifts
to Children's Law Center of
Los Angeles, Birthday Project,
201 Centre Plaza Drive, Suite 10,
Monterey Park, CA 91754-2178
(www.clcla.org).**

In Los Angeles County, more than twenty thousand children—victims of abuse and neglect—are placed in foster care. They are often moved from home to home and from school to school as many as a dozen times. In such a huge system, birthdays often fall through the cracks and can be especially sad. No party, no presents.

But Princess Ramey and her colleagues at the Children's Law Center of Los Angeles are changing that. Princess is an attorney and children's advocate, protecting the rights of children in troubled families. She oversees "The Birthday Project," collecting new toys, books, cosmetics, and gift certificates so foster children can have happy birthdays too.

Students at Crossroads Middle School for Arts and Sciences in Santa Monica, California, created seven hundred birthday bags filled with gifts for the

Do One Nice Thing

Children's Law Center. Gifts included coloring books with crayons, Hot Wheels, dolls, Legos, Etch A Sketches, disposable cameras with small photo albums, board games, and balls. Also included in the bags were balloons, notes of encouragement, and handmade pictures.

What can you, a child in your life, or your local school do that's like this? I bet whatever you dream up will be special.

••••••••••••••••••••••••

"Most of us remember a birthday when we felt as if we were the center of attention, our futures were as bright as the candles on our birthday cake, and at least for that day or that moment, our wishes might be granted. Unfortunately many children in foster care have nothing to unwrap, no candles to blow out, and often no one to wish them a happy birthday. The Birthday Project attempts to ensure that all children in foster care will be able to celebrate their birthdays."—Princess

Debbie Tenzer

BookEnds

**Send a new or gently used
children's book to BookEnds,
6520 Platt Avenue, Suite 331,
West Hills, CA 91307.**

The Ballad of BookEnds

Brandon had the sniffles and was watching TV,
When Mom said, "I have a meeting. Please come with me."

At the meeting he heard something so cruel;
There were no books for an orphans' school.

Couldn't they buy some? "Too expensive!" folks cried,
Then Brandon got an idea and felt happy inside.

The next day at his school he put up his hand,
And told his class about his big plan.

"What if we donate *our* books, the ones that we've read?
Don't clog up your closets. Help orphans instead."

His friends shouted *hooray!* And all agreed
To bring their books to Brandon and follow his lead.

*Harry Potter, Mother Goose, Green Eggs and Ham,
The Little Engine That Could,* I think I can I think I can!

Do One Nice Thing

More than eight hundred books, a sight to behold;
All because of Brandon who was eight years old.

When his mom saw the boxes she felt so proud,
"We'll make this permanent," she pledged aloud.

So BookEnds was born from Brandon's good deed,
To teach kids to help, and help kids to read.

Now at the orphanage, you can hear the kids' laughter;
They're reading books . . . happily ever after.

BookEnds is making a fantastic impact on hundreds of thousands of children:

→ More than 140,000 student volunteers have collected used books through events that they organized, and then delivered the books to needy schools and youth organizations.

→ More than 1.5 million books have been given away.

→ More than 400,000 at-risk kids have received books.

It really was the idea of an eight-year-old boy named Brandon. His mom, Robin Keefe, is BookEnds founder and president. Take a peek at BookEnds.org and help kids get hooked on reading.

Debbie Tenzer

Read a Book,
Get a Sticker

Send stickers to children in African villages. Images on the stickers can be geometric shapes, stars, animals, or castles, but please avoid violent images and cartoon characters. The more glittery, the better! Mail to Friends of African Village Libraries, PO Box 90533, San Jose, CA 95109-3533.

What would your life be like if the only books you'd ever seen were textbooks and assignment books in school? What if you'd never read a book for fun? No nursery rhymes, no poetry, no stories.

Michael Kevane, an economist, and Leslie Gray, a geographer, thought about that. They are a husband-and-wife team who teach at Santa Clara University in California. While doing research in the small African country of Burkina Faso, they discovered that rural schools had few books, and there were no libraries at all. So they raised funds to build a library in the small village where they were working, and eventually

Do One Nice Thing

launched nine more libraries in Burkina Faso, Ghana, Tanzania, and Uganda.

Now schoolchildren come to the library and read books for fun—a new concept for them. Stickers are handed out during Story Hour, a popular innovation, and are displayed on posters to show how many books a child reads, or how often they come to the library.

Adults benefit too. Local farmers, craftspeople, and traders come to the library seeking information on everything from dysentery to chicken coops. Libraries also provide employment for educated men and women who cannot find jobs that make use of their training. And sometimes a woman slips into the library from the fields, whispering, "Teach me to read."

....

"I enjoy reading novels and legends about Africa because they help connect us to our past. History is my favorite subject at school, because we can learn so much from things that have already happened."—Ini Kambiré, fourteen, who plans to become a nurse

Debbie Tenzer

Little Helping Hands

Teach your children empathy by taking them with you to check on an elderly neighbor and help at his or her home.

Bring in or take out the garbage cans.
Rake the leaves.
Wash the car.
Help in the garden.
Bake and deliver some cookies.
Shovel snow.
Or just say "hello"!

Officer Rob Zeeb is a patrol officer with the Brea Police Department in Southern California. He is also a school resource officer and one of the principal creators of the Brea P.D.'s S.A.F.E. Program—Skills and Assets for Excellence. The program encourages elementary school students to perform at least one hour of community service each week. Since the program began a few years ago, thousands of elementary school students have participated.

Some of the projects have included creating and performing a holiday program at a senior citizens'

Do One Nice Thing

home, collecting canned food items for local food banks, mentoring younger students at their schools and churches, helping school custodians, babysitting for free, walking elderly neighbors' dogs, and picking up trash around the community.

After nine weeks, Officer Zeeb and his colleagues hold a "graduation" and give an award to each student who fulfilled their commitment of giving an hour per week. In this way the children are acknowledged for helping others and developing a sense of responsibility for their community. The SAFE program has been so successful that other police departments and school districts have purchased the curriculum to use in their communities.

....

"We went to deliver groceries to a lady, and her nurse came to the door. She invited us in to meet the lady. We met her and she was so nice! She said thank-you to us and gave us chocolate lollipops. It made me feel good and happy that I helped someone. And I got chocolate!"—Maddy, age ten

Debbie Tenzer

Horses in the Hood

Send a new disposable camera so campers can take photos of their wonderful week at horse camp. Send cameras to Horses in the Hood, c/o Mill Creek Equestrian Center, 1881 Old Topanga Canyon Rd., Topanga, CA 90290.

Kathy Kusner is a pioneer. A champion equestrian and Olympic medalist, she was also the first licensed female jockey in the United States. In 1999 she set her sights on a different hurdle: inner-city violence in South Central Los Angeles. She wanted to give children a respite from it, so she founded Horses in the Hood, a nonprofit organization that provides amazing one-week horse-camp experiences.

The camp's mission is to introduce children to the joy of riding and caring for horses. Kids get to spend a week at this idyllic camp near the Pacific Ocean. For some, the bus ride to camp is the first time they've ever seen the ocean, although it's just a few miles from their homes. Over the course of the week, the children improve their communication skills and

Do One Nice Thing

develop a sense of responsibility, both necessary for good horsemanship. And it's fun!

••••••••••••••••••••••••

"When we first arrived at horse camp, the students were a little intimidated by the horses. And I have to admit; I was just as scared as they were. I had never been around a horse in my life and can't even begin to imagine how my students felt the first time they stared upward at this huge yet gentle animal, which towered above them. Shortly thereafter, the staff made everyone feel confident around these beautiful creatures, and soon enough we were riding.

"I was very surprised to see how quickly the students took to the care of the horses' everyday needs. Watching children who had never even seen a horse, brush, bathe, clean the horses' feet, and put the horse back in its stall was truly amazing. Each student took great care and love assuring that his or her horse was properly maintained. It just goes to show that if given an opportunity, children will surprise you every time."—Latonya, a school counselor

Debbie Tenzer

Everybody Up!

Children need to exercise more (don't we all!). Do a nice thing for them. When they're watching television, ask them to get up and walk in place whenever a commercial is on. Every little bit helps.

An hour-long television show typically contains about sixteen minutes of ads and announcements. That got me thinking: Kids watch on average four hours of TV daily. That equals more than *an hour* of commercials—a big chunk of time that kids could be walking, running, or dancing in place.

Get 'em up! Who knows? Maybe they'll enjoy it so much that they'll keep moving throughout the rest of the show. Or better yet, maybe they'll turn off the tube and dance to some music or run outside to play.

This "nice thing" works for grown-ups too. You don't need a gym membership to burn off calories. Just stand up and move a little—you don't even have to miss your favorite shows.

Do One Nice Thing

Flight Delays

Got a few minutes (or hours) to spare in an airport? Help your kids amuse themselves by making colorful letters for grandparents and friends. They can write thank-you notes after a visit or draw pictures of their experience. Pack paper and markers, and you're good to go. Then mail the letters from your destination.

While waiting, if your children finish all the thank-you notes they need to write, help them start a "card business." They can make cards that you can send for future birthdays, Christmas, Hanukkah, Thanksgiving, and every other holiday. On the back of each card they can sign their names: "Made by Lily with love."

Lucky you! You won't have to buy cards for a long time, and the recipients will cherish your child's custom artwork more than any store-bought greeting.

Debbie Tenzer

Less Is More

After your child's next birthday party, teach her or him to select a present or two to give to a homeless shelter for a needy child to enjoy.

How many birthday presents does a child appreciate? Most children can't wait to rip open the wrapping of their gifts. But afterward what happens? Kids usually play with just a few presents and ignore the rest. This is especially true of very young children. What a waste.

PhilaShelter (Northwest Philadelphia Interfaith Hospitality Network) is a group of Philadelphia churches and synagogues that come together to host homeless families. For them, "Love your neighbor as yourself" is real. The families are called guests and are treated to home-cooked meals and a place to sleep. Guests rotate from congregation to congregation and receive advice on jobs, parenting, and finances.

....

"Dear Do One Nice Thing, we thank you for your carefully selected gifts for our children and families. We have been having lots of fun with each mail delivery

Do One Nice Thing

and have received packages and good wishes from so many people and places. We are using the items for welcome kits for new families joining our program."
—PhilaShelter

....

PhilaShelter guests would enjoy small toys, decks of cards, sewing kits, and art supplies. Mail to NPIHN, 7047 Germantown Avenue, Philadelphia, PA 19119.

Debbie Tenzer

"I Love You" in Swahili

Send a pair of flip-flops or other sandals, any size, to the TunaHAKI kids: TunaHAKI Center, PO Box 1284, Moshi, Kilimanjaro, Tanzania. Shipping instructions: On the customs form, write *Donation for orphanage; no commercial value.*

Once upon a time, Scott Fifer was strictly a Hollywood TV and film writer. He wrote for the Emmy Awards, Radio Music Awards, *Beverly Hills 90210,* and many other popular shows.

One Christmas he decided to take a "volunteer vacation" that he had read about on the Internet. He spent a month in Tanzania, where he helped a group of street kids living at a shelter called the TunaHAKI Center. The name means "We have a RIGHT" in Swahili. There is no running water, and the children, all orphaned or abandoned, sleep two or three to a bed. But they have a roof over their heads and receive food, clothing, education, medical care, and instruction in the arts. They also learn acrobatics.

Do One Nice Thing

Scott fell in love with the kids, who were outgoing, sweet, and energetic. He taught them English, and they taught him Swahili. (*Nakupenda* means "I love you.") Together they went on field trips around town. He marveled at the group's acrobatic skills, which were so good that the kids performed for tourists at nearby hotels and then passed the hat for donations to pay for food and school fees.

The trip changed Scott. When he returned to California, he didn't feel like writing jokes for award shows anymore. Instead, without any prior knowledge of how to do it, he founded a nonprofit organization to help the children—the TunaHAKI Foundation.

Scott pays for all fund-raising and administrative expenses out of his own pocket so that 100 percent of all donations go directly to benefit the kids. Now, under Scott's guidance, a permanent home, vocational school, and training center are being built on three acres in Tanzania for the kids. There will be a self-supporting poultry farm and housing for one hundred children too.

"I was born thirteen years ago. I was obtained by Tuna-HAKI at a bus stand. My mother had mental illness. She left me at the bus stop one day and ordered me to wait there until she returned. I waited for one week, but she

Debbie Tenzer

never came back. I am now an artist performing acrobatics and dance throughout the local community. I like TunaHAKI because it gives me food and it makes me feel good when people clap."—Colman

●●●●●●●●●●●●●●●●●●●●●●●●●●

"I can't comprehend how the work I have done personally affects the kids at TunaHAKI. We don't talk about it and I don't ask or even think about it. But once in a while I let myself step back, and I see it in their smiles. And those smiles are gratifying."—Scott

Do One Nice Thing

You've Been Accepted

**Help students go to college.
Donate a new or gently used SAT
or college guide book to a local
high school for students who can't
afford them.**

Kristina Schwartz has advised thousands of high school students on how to get into college. From her many years of experience, she knows what colleges are seeking, and this makes her guidance outstanding. But she is no ordinary college counselor. She's more like an exuberant coach.

While other counselors probe students about their grades, courses, and test scores, Kristina's mind is speeding in a completely different direction. She explained: "I need to find out what's cool about a kid. Kids are under a lot of pressure. Some have been told that they won't succeed, but I never believe it. Every kid is amazing in some way. I try to give kids the courage to go out into the world and do what *they* want to do."

Her students say she always treats them with respect, and she really listens to what they say. One of her former students remembered Kristina this way:

Debbie Tenzer

"Another counselor said that the university I dreamed of attending was out of reach for me. But Kristina understood how much I cared about it, so she encouraged me to apply anyway. She said, 'We're going to do this together, and we're going to do our very best.'

"That's what we did, and incredibly, I was accepted! Going to college there was fantastic. Those four years gave me not only a great education, but some of my best friends and lots of really wonderful memories. When I think back on it, I'm still amazed by the whole thing. Without Kristina, it wouldn't have happened. She made me feel that anything was possible, and now I believe it."

Do One Nice Thing

Dear Santa

Become "Santa" by answering a letter and making a needy child's Christmas dream come true. In November and December, request a "Dear Santa" letter from your local post office.

Each year a million children write letters to Santa Claus requesting gifts for Christmas. Many of their parents secretly buy and wrap gifts to fulfill their children's dreams. But for hundreds of thousands of children, no gifts arrive for Christmas because their parents cannot afford to buy them. Fortunately, many "Dear Santa" letters reach the U.S. Postal Service, where mail carriers, on their own time, organize the letters and make them available to the public to help.

When Landon was eleven years old, his parents, Wendi and Will, obtained a "Dear Santa" letter. It was written by a woman who lived with her elderly aunt and five children of various ages in a dangerous neighborhood in Los Angeles. The children were her nieces, nephews, and grandchildren, ages three to eighteen.

Debbie Tenzer

She had taken them in because their parents had died or were otherwise unable to care for them.

The letter to Santa requested clothes for the kids—a sweater, a pair of shoes, things that Landon had considered necessities, not presents. He picked out some barely worn clothes of his own to give, and he and Wendi bought toys too—something for each person mentioned in the letter. Then Landon and Wendi lovingly wrapped all the gifts and included a letter, wishing them Merry Christmas "from Santa."

How will you know if someone asking for presents really needs them? A service representative at my local post office told me that mail carriers read all the "Dear Santa" letters to determine which children truly need gifts. After all, mail carriers know every home in every neighborhood. They contribute gifts "from Santa" too.

• • • • • • • • • • • • • • • • •

"We wanted our son to understand that the things we take for granted are treasured by someone else. The experience itself was a gift for him."—Wendi

Do One Nice Thing

3

Do One Nice Thing for Pets and the Planet

"Look around you. At the end of the day, we must leave our campsite cleaner than we found it." That's how the camp leader welcomed us on our first day of Girl Scout Summer Camp near Oakland, California. I was five years old, and I still remember it.

My little friends and I peered at the sunshine spilling through towering trees and we inhaled the fragrances of wildflowers, honeysuckle, and pine. It was silent except for a trickling stream and the sweet melodies of birds. What a magnificent place!

That day the wise camp leader didn't simply say, "Keep it clean." Instead, the first thing she did was make us look—truly look—at how beautiful the campsite was. She knew that if we appreciated what we had, then we would feel duty-bound to take care of it.

Today we all know that "our campsite" isn't as clean as it should be. The planet is in serious condition. We know we need to consume less and recycle more. The question is, How? It's not as simple anymore as picking up the trash at the end of the day—although that helps too.

Who doesn't want to conserve energy and reduce air pollution? We all do, but not all of us are able to carpool, walk, or bike to work. Or have the funds to replace our appliances and cars with new energy-efficient models. Or have the time or space to hang out our laundry to dry on a clothesline.

If you can do those things, that's admirable. But if you can't, don't give up. This chapter will present some easy ways to reduce waste, save trees, reuse materials in our homes, and protect animals. If all of us do what we can, we'll be able to clean up this planet—one campsite at a time.

Debbie Tenzer

Home Sweet Home

**Become a foster parent for a pet.
Pet parents are needed to provide
a temporary home for kittens,
puppies, or other animals in need
(www.pets911.com/services/foster).**

Animal shelters simply cannot cope with the number
of animals who need housing. Some animals are suffering from stress, illness, or trauma, or are just very
young. They can recover and grow strong if they receive a family's tender loving care.

Also, please spay or neuter your pet. One female
dog and her offspring can produce 67,000 puppies in
six years. One female cat and her offspring can produce 420,000 kittens in seven years.

....

"Taking in foster animals is a great activity for the entire family. I have taken in unwanted puppies and kittens from local shelters for a few days or weeks until
they are well and old enough to go to permanent
homes. My children are learning from the experience
too."—Diane

Do One Nice Thing

Your New Baby Panda

"Adopt" an endangered animal through the World Wildlife Fund. By protecting pandas, gorillas, tigers, and other animals, you will protect additional species that live in the same habitats. You will also improve the lives of poor rural people who live nearby. When habitats become healthier, humans become healthier too.

Symbolically adopting an endangered animal is a wonderful project to do with children. When my daughter was eight, her class studied endangered animals. Each child chose an animal to research, and my daughter chose the giant panda. We visited the World Wildlife Fund website and "adopted" a panda.

Our family has been in love with pandas ever since. We trekked to the San Diego Zoo to see the pandas on loan from China, and there was great excitement because after many years of pandas failing to reproduce, a new baby panda had recently been born.

After waiting in line at the exhibit for over an hour, we were rewarded by seeing little Hua Mei

Debbie Tenzer

wake up from a nap and nuzzle with her huge, gentle mother, Bai Yun. Hua Mei was the first giant panda born in North America to survive to adulthood. She has since returned to China and given birth to three sets of twins.

You can visit the pandas at the San Diego Zoo anytime by watching the zoo's "Panda Cam" (www .sandiegozoo.org/zoo/ex_panda_station.html).

Do One Nice Thing

Dogs and Their People Who Save Lives

**Help abandoned animals: To
donate free food for them, just click
www.TheAnimalRescueSite.com.**

We love our pets, but Lee Haus's dog, Brutus, is more than a pet—he is her partner. Together, they are an emergency response team with Los Angeles' search and rescue task force. When disaster strikes anywhere in the United States, Lee, Brutus, and their colleagues calmly move in, focused on saving lives.

Brutus came to Lee from the Search Dog Foundation, a nonprofit group that provides the country's most highly trained search dogs, and partners them with firefighters and other first responders. SDF's extraordinary dogs and handlers participated in recovery efforts at the World Trade Center site following the September 11 attacks. They also worked in the areas hit by Hurricanes Ike, Gustav, Katrina, and Rita, as well as other disaster sites.

Most of SDF's rescue dogs were rescued themselves. Abused or abandoned, the dogs are taken in by SDF, which trains them and takes care of them for life. When dogs cannot search anymore due to age or

Debbie Tenzer

injury, they remain with their handlers or SDF finds good homes for them.

For Lee the best part of the job is watching Brutus search. "It's amazing how he figures it out, no matter how deep he needs to dig or how many distractions there are around him. He'll run, stop, turn, and then go to work."

Lee described their experience in Louisiana following Hurricane Rita: "We were searching a part of the New Orleans Parish that had flooded up to the eaves of the houses. Our mission was to go house to house and search for survivors. It was 101 degrees with 85 percent humidity, and we were searching eight hours a day. There was mud everywhere—in some places, up to our thighs. The houses were full of debris and furniture was toppled everywhere. We kicked, crawled, slipped, and pushed our way into each house. Our dogs worked like champs, always willing. It was great to put all my training with my pup to work."

What will happen when Brutus retires? Lee says, "We'll be together. We're a team." For life.

Do One Nice Thing

Best Friends

Donate unused or gently used pet toys, dishes, beds, and other pet items to your local animal shelter or to Best Friends Animal Society and Sanctuary, 5001 Angel Canyon Road, Kanab, UT 84741 (www.BestFriends.org).

If your pet passes away, this is a wonderful way to extend your love by comforting a needy animal. You can also purchase pet toys and treats online to donate to Best Friends.

It's a jungle out there, and sadly, many helpless animals are left alone to fend for themselves. Best Friends Animal Sanctuary, the largest animal sanctuary in the United States, protects more than two thousand dogs, cats, and other animals every day. Some of them arrive from shelters across the United States due to storms, floods, fires, and neglect, while others have been rescued from as far away as Lebanon.

After receiving some tender loving care, many of the animals are adopted by loving families. But for an-

Debbie Tenzer

imals that are too old, ill, or traumatized to move on, Best Friends becomes their new home. Residents include birds, pigs, rabbits, horses, burros, mules, goats, ducks, snakes, squirrels, and, of course, dogs and cats.

The sanctuary also welcomes about twenty thousand humans each year, who are allowed to feed and groom the animals, play with them, as well as take them on walks. If you are planning a trip to southern Utah, stop in and be prepared to fall in love with Best Friends' sweet creatures. Maybe one of them will love you back, and you'll add a new member to your family.

• •

"A dog is the only thing on earth that loves you more than he loves himself."—Josh Billings

Do One Nice Thing

Free Kibble

Donate free dog and cat food to abandoned animals by playing the Bow Wow Dog Trivia game at www.FreeKibble.com.

What is the favorite dog breed in the United States? Labrador Retriever!

Twelve-year-old Mimi Ausland loves animals. She wanted to find a way to feed abandoned dogs at her local humane society in Oregon. So she came up with an idea with her mom and dad: a dog trivia game on a website. What if every time a person played, ad revenue was generated to buy free kibble for needy dogs?

Why was the poodle haircut invented? So poodles could swim more easily!

It worked. Local businesses signed on to help, and FreeKibble.com was born. Play every day. Whether your answer is right or wrong, free food will be donated to abandoned animals at the Humane Society of Central Oregon.

Mimi and her parents hope to grow the site so they'll be able to provide kibble to animal shelters in other places, too. There are tens of thousands of hungry dogs in shelters across the United States, so Mimi

Debbie Tenzer

is busy. She's talking to classes, participating in events with the Humane Society, and doing other community projects to encourage people to help animals.

After seeing how popular FreeKibble.com became, Mimi also launched the Meow Cat Trivia game at www.FreeKibbleKat.com so she can feed abandoned cats too.

How many people does it take to make a difference? Just one. You!

．．．．．．．．．．．．．．．．．．．．．．．

"I absolutely *love* delivering the food to the Humane Society! Before our first delivery, FreeKibble.com was just a website with virtual kibble. But when we went out to deliver food for the first time, I got to put the bags of kibble in the storage room, feed the dogs, and play with them. I then realized that by feeding the dogs here and other places, the shelters can use that money to get the animals more toys, cat food, litter boxes, leashes, food bowls, and more. So after that day of delivering food to hungry dogs, FreeKibble.com was real!"—Mimi

Do One Nice Thing

Love from a Wet Nose

**Be a puppy sitter. Weekend
volunteers help socialize
puppies that are being raised
to become service dogs.
Send an e-mail to programs@
puppiesbehindbars.com or visit
www.puppiesbehindbars.com.**

Puppies Behind Bars trains prison inmates to raise
puppies to become service dogs. Their handlers learn
to contribute to society and feel human again while
preparing the dogs to help disabled children and adults,
and veterans returning from Iraq and Afghanistan.
Some dogs also assist police and international security
forces with explosives detection.

Volunteer puppy sitters are needed to socialize the
puppies during their weekend "furloughs." This is because service dogs need to acclimate to various envi-
ronments and stress levels. So they need to experience
going into stores and restaurants, walking on different
streets, attending softball and soccer games, as well as
other activities.

On weekends, puppies also visit homebound elderly senior citizens in New York City. Puppies learn

Debbie Tenzer

from their interaction with people, and seniors who rarely leave their apartments love to receive puppy kisses.

How many people's lives are transformed by Puppies Behind Bars? Prison inmates, home-bound elderly people, countless people in public venues, disabled children and adults, and veterans and their families. And every puppy needs to be socialized by a volunteer. Could that be you?

Do One Nice Thing

A Partridge in a Pear Tree

Give away holiday decorations you don't use.

Do you have old holiday decorations that are gathering dust in a closet? Give them away and spread the holiday spirit. You could also

- → get together with friends to swap Christmas ornaments
- → donate ornaments to your local shelter. They will give the rooms a lovely holiday feeling.
- → ask local clergy if someone who can't afford decorations would like to receive yours. Can you donate a Christmas tree too?

· ·

"I gave away the holiday decorations that I didn't use this year. I filled a box of things to give to my friends who don't have as much as I do."—Barbara

Debbie Tenzer

What's in Your Wallet?

Send your used gift cards, identity, hotel, library and other plastic cards to be recycled. Cut them in half and mail to Earthworks System, c/o Halperin Industries, 25840 Miles Road, Bedford, OH 44146.

Do you ever wonder what happens to all those gift cards and other plastic cards when you're done with them? Billions of them are produced every year, and eventually they all end up in landfills . . . *forever.* These cards are made of polyvinyl chloride (PVC), which is not biodegradable, and even worse, it contains petroleum and other nasty chemicals that leach into the earth. Yuck.

Fortunately, the smart people at Earthworks System created a solution. They melt down the old cards and transform them into new cards. The recycled cards are made with 80 percent less energy than brand-new ones, and without any petroleum.

. . . .

"I love to recycle. I work in a hair salon and always try to bring new ideas to my clients, so I gave them the address to send all their old gift cards to. I figure any small thing I can do helps."—Lori

Do One Nice Thing

Big Turnoff

Turn off the following:

→ your lights and everything else in a room when you leave it

→ your computer each night

→ your car engine when waiting longer than 10 seconds

→ your shower, sooner

→ and unplug appliances, when practical, so they don't drain electricity when not in use

You know what to do, but a little reminder couldn't hurt, right?

If you need some help around the house, I've found that kids are very effective "energy cops" and will happily inspect your home to turn off the lights, televisions, and radios that a goofy grown-up left on accidentally. Giving them this job will teach them responsibility as well as good conservation habits. They can even make an Energy Star calendar and reward you with stars for the days that you remember to turn everything off.

Debbie Tenzer

"I read that 40 percent of our energy bill is due to appliances left plugged in even when turned off. So now I make sure the toaster, lamps, and anything else with a plug is unplugged when not in use. Yes, it is a huge change and maybe even an inconvenience, but that extra second I spend is a huge step in reducing the energy I consume. Every time I unplug an appliance or lamp, I am conscious of our fragile planet and the little steps it takes to conserve energy."—Sue

Do One Nice Thing

Nice Things Happen in the Dark

Pick a time that's convenient for you on Monday nights and turn off your lights for an hour.

→ Dine by candlelight.

→ Read by flashlight.

→ Prepare a cold dinner.

→ Sit outside and gaze at the stars.

→ Take a stroll.

What was life like a hundred years ago when there were no energy-guzzling conveniences? Pretend for an hour each week: Reduce your energy usage and give Mother Earth a rest.

On March 31, 2007, families, businesses, and government groups in Sydney, Australia, banded together to reduce global warming in a simple, wonderful way. They switched off their lights. For an hour on that Saturday night, dubbed "Earth Hour," office buildings stopped providing light to workers who weren't there, lit-up monuments went dark, and restaurant patrons ate by candlelight. By doing so, the people of

Debbie Tenzer

Sydney reduced emissions equivalent to the exhaust from 48,000 cars. And they did it in just one hour.

For Earth Hour the following year, Sydney did even better and was joined by 370 towns, cities, and municipalities around the globe. In Los Angeles, my husband and I turned off the lights in our home and ate dinner by candlelight. We felt connected to millions of people worldwide who were participating that night, all doing our part to make the planet healthier. Plus, a romantic dinner is a very nice thing.

Do One Nice Thing

Got Silk?

Recycle your leftover fabric, yarn, and paper to make heartfelt cards and gifts.

Transform your clothing scraps, magazines, art supplies, and cards into creative tools. Use them to design colorful bookmarks, collages, and festive birthday and holiday cards. You can also fashion bright "vases" from frozen juice containers and milk cartons.

••••••••••••••••••••••

"I use the 'less desirable' colors (the seventies olive, brown, and gold, for example) and styles of yarn and fabric to make pet mats for animal shelters and rescue groups. A dog or cat isn't especially fussy about colors, if they can be comfortable while in a cage waiting for adoption."—Marsha

••••••••••••••••••••••

"My daughter saved soup cans and had her church and Brownie Scout craft groups make pencil holders, which were great looking."—Sandy

Debbie Tenzer

Three Ways to Save Trees

Take the Cash

Every time I use an ATM, I notice that the nearby garbage can is full of discarded receipts. What a waste. There are *billions* of Automatic Teller Machine (ATM) transactions in the United States each year. If everyone would opt not to get a receipt, think of all the trees we'd save. Instead, take a moment to record your transaction in your checkbook.

Junk Removal

Are you tired of tossing out half the mail you receive, all those envelopes that you never wanted in the first place? A lot of trees were cut down to make that garbage.

There's something you can do about it. Delete your name and address from some of the senders' mailing lists. It's easy to do on the Direct Marketing Association website: https://www.dmachoice.org. Removing your name won't eliminate all of your junk mail, but it should reduce it.

Do One Nice Thing

Stamp 'Em Out

Get rid of paper bills. Pay your bills online instead. It's easy to set up with your bank. Then your mail can't get lost, you'll save paper, and you'll use many fewer stamps. And best of all, you can pay at the very last minute.

Debbie Tenzer

Eat Your Veggies

Once a week eat a meatless meal.

When was the last time you hung out with some cows? *Yow!* They give the term air pollution a whole new meaning.

When my family drives on Highway 5 between Northern and Southern California, we pass a large cattle ranch. Actually, we know well in advance when we're approaching the ranch. Windows *up,* please. This is not only a temporary olfactory nuisance. Livestock farming—specifically the manure from it—is a major source of greenhouse-gas emissions.

So how about trying a nonmeat, nondairy meal once a week? Just once! You will also do a nice thing for your arteries by lowering your cholesterol intake. Here are some easy-to-prepare ideas from my kitchen. I invite you to create your own.

Mango-Cashew Salad: Combine a chopped head of romaine lettuce, a peeled and chopped jicama, a sliced scallion, ½ cup dried cranberries, a peeled and diced mango, 1 cup cashews, and 1 tablespoon raspberry dressing to moisten.

Do One Nice Thing

Fish Amandine: Sauté sliced almonds, sliced mushrooms, a minced clove of garlic, and scallions in olive oil. Spoon over any kind of broiled fish.

California Couscous: Stir together couscous as prepared from a box, 1 cup orange juice, a handful of chopped parsley, 1 cup garbanzo beans, ½ cup currants or raisins, and 1 teaspoon cinnamon. Refrigerate for 2 hours before serving.

Debbie Tenzer

Let's Go Shopping

Buy Big

Reduce waste by buying products in bulk and the largest size that is reasonable for your needs. One big box, bag, or container uses less packaging than three smaller ones.

Buy Less

Instead of buying CDs, download music on your computer. CD jewel cases are made from polyvinyl chloride (PVC), a material that is extremely difficult to recycle and is associated with numerous health risks.

Buy Local

When you're shopping for produce, find out where it came from. When we import food from halfway around the world, we are also importing air pollution from the airplanes, trucks, and ships that bring the food to us. By buying local produce in season, you'll reduce air pollution, support farmers nearby, and enjoy fresher, tastier food.

Do One Nice Thing

Buy Recyclables

Choose paper napkins that have a high recycled content. If every home in the United States replaced *just one package* of virgin fiber napkins with 100 percent recycled ones, it's estimated that we could save one million trees.

. . . .

"I bring my own cloth bags to the grocery store."
—Laura

Debbie Tenzer

Never Throw Away Anything

**Swap goods for free on
www.freecycle.org.**

The Freecycle Network is a group of more than five million people around the world who try really hard not to throw things away. Instead, they swap with or give them to someone who wants them. The Freecycle website lists local groups so Freecyclers can find each other online.

••••••••••••••••••••••••

"I belong to local Freecycle groups, which donate items to those who have a need. You can post an offer or a wanted ad and then make arrangements to deliver or pick the items up. It's a great way to discard things you wouldn't want thrown in the trash, and someone who needs them benefits. One (wo)man's trash is another's treasure!"—Rebecca

Do One Nice Thing

4

Do One Nice Thing That Heals

Illness humbles us. Whether it happens to us or someone close to us, it reminds us that we don't have as much control over life as we like to think. And that's scary.

When someone we care about is sick, many of us feel so helpless, we don't know what to do. Healing moves at its own pace. Slowly. A little at a time. At times the frustration that comes with it can be overwhelming. Yet affection, encouragement, kindness, and laughter are powerful medicines. They can make the journey easier for the patient, as well as the wide web of friends and family who are also affected by the illness.

A card, a call, a hug, a reminder that "I'm proud of you"—all of these soothe and remind someone that they are not alone. Here are some ways that you can help someone heal, whether it's someone you know or just another member of our human family.

Debbie Tenzer

Operation Feel Better

Mail a get-well card in care of the Volunteers Department to your local children's hospital or the pediatric department of a hospital. Addresses are available at www.childrenshospitals.net; click on the link About Children's Hospitals.

Imagine a frightened child lying in a hospital bed, away from her home and everything that's familiar to her. Now imagine the smile on that child's face—and on the faces of her worried parents and grandparents—when they see a card, handmade by a stranger. That stranger can be you.

Making a get-well card for a hospitalized child is a wonderful project to do with children or with friends. Take a piece of paper. Write "You're so strong," "I'm proud of you!," "You're terrific!" and similar messages. Decorate with hearts, smiley faces, rainbows, or whatever you like, and seal it with a kiss.

Please avoid using glitter and other small objects that could accidentally end up in a young child's mouth or eyes.

Do One Nice Thing

"My name is Reina and I am a student in Los Angeles. For my 'Sweet Sixteen' party, I decided to have my guests participate in an activity I love to do. I had them make cards for Do One Nice Thing's Operation Feel Better. This way I would share the joy I felt on my special day.

"We ended up making 101 cards in total! Completing all the cards was one of the highlights of my summer. I hope these cards will brighten the day of patients and their families in need of cheering up."

"Thank you for your recent donation of handmade greeting cards. This is a wonderful project and we are delighted to be included. The cards were sent out on meal trays as tray favors. The children were very happy to receive them, and we thank you for helping make their hospital stay a little more enjoyable. We would love to have more cards!"—Miami Children's Hospital

Debbie Tenzer

Kid Flicks

**Do you have children's DVDs?
You can do a double-nice thing by
recycling them and donating them
to Kid Flicks. Send them to: Kid
Flicks/Barta, 11755 Wilshire
Boulevard, Suite 1450, Los Angeles,
CA 90025.**

Meet a brilliant medical team: Dr. H. Potter, Dr. M. Pop-
pins, Dr. W. T. Pooh, Dr. L. Mermaid.

Kid Flicks collects children's movies and donates
them to children's hospitals and pediatric departments all over the U.S. It was founded by four girls—
the Barta sisters—in Los Angeles. But after two left
for college, the youngest two, Berni and Marni, took
over the organization.

The idea for Kid Flicks emerged a few years ago
when the girls visited one of their young friends who
was being treated for leukemia in the hospital. While
she was receiving chemotherapy, she would watch
movies to pass the time and distract her from the dis-
comfort.

This gave the Bartas an idea. The next time they
came to visit, they brought some of their videos and

Do One Nice Thing

DVDs. The movies were so popular that the girls decided to collect as many as possible to donate to hospitals for kids. They told a few people, and within a week they'd collected 100 movies.

That was almost seven years ago. Now they've collected more than *35,000 movies.* It would be wonderful if the girls simply collected and sent out the movies to hospitals, but they do even more. They assemble 100 assorted films to create a "film library," so a hospital receives a collection of films that children of various ages and interests can enjoy.

And that is what they are still doing today: lovingly collecting and donating film libraries, systematically contacting hospitals, and inspiring people to give them their used DVDs. So far they have donated more than 350 film libraries. But the number of sick children Berni and Marni have touched, and the anxieties they have eased, is uncountable.

How many teens have the imagination, maturity, and compassion to create and execute a project like this? How many adults do?

••••••••••••••••••••••••••

"One of the things about Kid Flicks that makes us feel the best is how so many people contact us who are eager to get involved and help others. It feels great that we can help them do this. Not only do we get do-

Debbie Tenzer

nations from generous individuals from all over the country, but a lot of people have felt inspired to start their own Kid Flicks drives."—Marni and Berni

•••••••••••••••••••••••

"I have a son who spent weeks at a time in the hospital, and the most effective way to keep him occupied and entertained was movies. It is an incredibly valuable service to everyone who gets to watch them."—Marie

Do One Nice Thing

Clowning Around

Send a bottle of bubbles for clown doctors to use when they cheer up hospitalized children. Mail to Big Apple Circus, ATTN: Michael Christensen, 505 Eighth Avenue, 19th floor, New York, NY 10018.

Clowns, the original stand-up comedians, have been cheering up people in every culture for centuries. Historically, they've jumped out of pies (really big pies), coaxed mean kings and chiefs to laugh (a tough audience), and helped people forget their troubles despite plagues, wars, and other challenges of biblical proportions (floods, pestilence, droughts—the usual).

They also master acrobatics, juggling, dance, mime, and stilt walking. Can you do all that? Great! Now try doing it in extra-large shoes.

There is a unique group of clowns who are even more extraordinary: The Big Apple Circus Clown Care performers, also known as Clown Doctors. They are specially trained to put smiles on the faces of hospitalized children and to calm their fears.

Debbie Tenzer

Dr. Doodle Doo! Paging Dr. Doodle Doo!

The program was started in 1986 in New York City by Big Apple Circus cofounder Michael Christensen. At the time, he put on a white coat, packed some rubber chickens in a medical bag, and headed to a hospital to cheer up kids.

Now ninety-two Big Apple Circus Clown Doctors in nineteen cities make hundreds of thousands of bedside visits each year. They perform for children in intensive care units, bone-marrow transplant centers, burn-treatment centers, pediatric AIDS units, emergency rooms, acute-care clinics, physical therapy units, and inpatient and outpatient facilities.

Dr. Bonehead, please call Dr. Ima Confused as soon as possible!

The Clown Doctors have a few tricks up their sleeves, literally. Their *very complicated* medical procedures include:

→ red-nose transplants

→ kitty cat scans

→ chocolate milk transfusions

→ plate-spinning platelet tests

→ bubble blowing

Do One Nice Thing

But the Clown Doctors' most successful treatment isn't complicated at all: laughter.

••••••••••••••••••••••••

"At one point early on a doctor looked at me and said, 'Clowns don't belong in the ICU.' I just looked at him and said, 'Neither do children.' "—Michael

••••••••••••••••••••••••

"That's the first time I've seen my child laugh since we've been here."—The mother of a hospitalized child

Debbie Tenzer

Every Little Knit Helps

**Knit booties, blankets, and hats
and send them to Stitches from
the Heart, 3316 Pico Boulevard,
Santa Monica, CA 90405.**

Many people jokingly complain that they have "nothing to wear," but for premature babies this is literally true. They are so tiny that very few clothes fit them. This is one more concern for babies' parents who have already been through so much.

Five years ago, Kathy Silverton read an article about this problem, and she decided to help. Whenever she had a few free minutes, she would knit booties, blankets, and hats for the babies. She told other knitters and crocheters, and they enthusiastically joined her. When an article was published about her in a local newspaper, more than a hundred women contacted her wanting to join the project.

She then founded Stitches from the Heart, a nonprofit organization devoted to creating and sending handmade clothes for premature babies and babies from impoverished families. Every item is created with tender loving care and pride, and volunteers sometimes attach their names to the items.

Do One Nice Thing

Kathy's website provides directions on how to knit little clothes for "preemies." The head of a full-term baby is approximately the size of a grapefruit. But a premature baby's head is the size of an orange, or even a lemon. Stitches volunteers knit these tiny hats as well as tiny booties, sweaters, and blankets.

•••••••••••••••••••••••

"Knitting for the babies is a win-win. The families are so grateful, and the women who knit love what they're doing. There are more than 14,000 knitters, and they're all making a gift for a child they'll never know. We've sent more than 500,000 tiny garments so far, and each one is a labor of love."—Kathy

•••••••••••••••••••••••

"Dear Stitches from the Heart Volunteers,
"One of your precious hats was given to my grand-daughter who was born in May. She was two months premature, weighing just 3 lbs., 11 oz. I am familiar with 'Stitches' because I teach needle arts, and some of my students donate blankets and hats. I never expected to be a recipient of one of those precious hats. Every hat makes a difference! Thank you, stitching angels."—Susan

Debbie Tenzer

"My Brain: It's My Second Favorite Organ."
—Woody Allen

What's #1? The heart! This entry is about both because healing the brain requires lots of heart. Send a deck of playing cards, a wood kit, a watercolor set, a package of colored pencils, a sketchbook, stamp pads/rubber stamps, a 100- to 300-piece jigsaw puzzle, or games like Scrabble, Trouble, Uno, Scattergories (new or gently used) to someone with a brain injury.

Mail to Inpatient Rehab Unit, 3 MB, St. Mary's Hospital, Mayo Clinic, 200 First Street SW, Rochester, MN 55905.

It takes courage to face life after a brain injury. You need someone to wash, dress, and feed you. You have

Do One Nice Thing

to learn to walk, talk, and swallow again, while you put your broken mind back in working order. Every day that's what millions of people must do due to stroke, combat injury, accident, or disease. Fortunately these days many patients make astonishing recoveries, but it takes hard work, guts, and a loving, skillful support team. You can't do it alone.

Equestrian and singer Cindy Howden was thrown from a horse, paralyzed, and unable to chew or speak. But with personal tenacity and the Mayo Clinic's top-notch care, she learned to walk again. She returned to school, became a vocational counselor, and now works with people with disabilities.

A recovering person's motivation is critical, but no one can navigate this path alone. Physicians, psychologists, nurses, therapists, and loved ones are all on the journey too. With steady patience and encouragement, they help the patient move beyond the shock, pain, and loneliness toward hope, gratitude, and pride.

. . . .

"For the first time in my life I can't solve a problem by working or studying or trying harder. I've become more spiritual. Having been to Hell and back, I have a quiet peace. I have now been given the faith that I had been seeking but hadn't quite grasped. I see that

Debbie Tenzer

at every turn I have been blessed. I can live with very little and be happy. At the beginning of my rehab, I was told that I would need to have patience and take joy in incremental improvements. I do that now. How incredibly lucky I am."—Jean

Do One Nice Thing

Locks of Love

Can you spare some hair? If you can and it's at least ten inches long, you can provide hair for a child suffering from medical hair loss by sending it to Locks of Love, 234 Southern Boulevard, West Palm Beach, FL 33405.

After spending thirty years in business, David Callihan decided to switch gears. So he and his family moved to Florida, and David became a teacher. He joined the faculty of DeSoto Middle School, where he teaches math and coaches basketball. He also grew his hair long "for personal reasons."

"After a year, my hair was pretty long. One day our principal and I were talking. Our school had just barely missed getting a 'B' grade on the Florida Comprehensive Assessment Tests"—the dreaded annual test that measures students' progress.

They cooked up a challenge: If the students achieved a "B" grade on the FCAT, David promised to shave his head in front of the entire student body. The students loved it. They studied hard and the FCAT results arrived:

Debbie Tenzer

For the first time since 2002, DeSoto Middle School got a B!

All eyes were on the school's closed-circuit television as a local hairdresser cut David's foot-long locks. His hair did not go to waste. He donated it to Locks of Love. The hairpieces, all made from human hair, help restore children's self-esteem and boost their self-confidence.

David believes that with continued hard work the students can do even better, and he's raising the stakes: If they get an A on the next FCAT, he will let them *color* his hair any color they want.

. . . .

"Till I saw information on Locks of Love, I was just wasting my hair by getting it cut two inches at a time. Here in India, it's taboo for a married lady to cut her hair when her husband is alive and to grow hair when he is dead. And no wife whose husband is alive wants her hair cut at any cost, even now. But I was surprised and happy when my wife offered her hair for Locks of Love."—Malladi (His daughter Lipi donated twenty-seven inches of her glorious hair. He, his wife, and his other daughters donated their hair too.)

Do One Nice Thing

Everyone Needs a Break

"Babysit" a sick friend so his or her spouse or child can get a haircut, go out for a cup of coffee, or tend to errands. The caregiver will be grateful for the chance to relax or get caught up, and will return feeling renewed, with more energy and patience.

An accident, a devastating illness, or a wound in battle can strike suddenly and affect an entire family. Many people who go home after a catastrophic illness or life change need twenty-four-hour companionship and supervision. Giving care is exhausting, stressful, and expensive for loved ones.

. . . .

"My mom had a massive stroke at fifty-one and is now at home with Dad. We all help—and struggle. It's amazing the things you can live through . . . as a patient and as a family member. Paying a visit, playing a game, having a cup of coffee, helping with an errand or a meal wouldn't seem like much. But being on the receiving end is huge."—Robin

Debbie Tenzer

It's Great to Hear Your Voice

Do you know someone who is receiving medical care out of town? Perhaps a family member of theirs is the patient?? If they don't have a cell phone or have only local service, phone bills can be very expensive, which can be one more thing to worry about.

Give them a phone card. Being able to talk to loved ones will comfort them when they need comfort most. You can provide even more encouragement by writing a loving message on the card.

....

"When my husband was undergoing cancer treat-ment out of town, a phone card was a wonderful gift. I could stay in touch with family and receive much needed moral support."—Annie

Do One Nice Thing

A Soothing Touch

More than 500,000 people in the United States receive medical treatment each year for burn injuries. The process of healing takes a long time, and it helps to record one's feelings. You can do a nice thing for a burn survivor by sending a blank journal. Send it to The Phoenix Society for Burn Survivors, 1835 R W Berends Drive SW, Grand Rapids, MI 49519-4955.

The phoenix is a dazzling mythical bird that lives five hundred years. When the end of its life approaches, it bursts into flames. But soon it rises again, even more radiant than before. The Phoenix Society of Burn Survivors takes its name and inspiration from the legend.

....

"When I was injured in a car accident, there was little support for burn survivors. I had to re-enter society alone, carrying the stigma of being severely disfigured. Through the help of family and loved ones, I was introduced to the director of Let's Face It, an or-

Debbie Tenzer

ganization for people with facial differences, who in turn introduced me to the Phoenix Society.

"Today, eighteen years later, I have found my own skin again, metaphorically and physically. More so than before the accident, I have learned to evolve and be grateful for who I am. When things are difficult, I find myself repeating, 'It is what it is,' and in the same breath I say, 'It is all good.' "—Lily

Do One Nice Thing

It's a Bird! It's a Plane! It's a Nice-o-holic!

Skydive for breast cancer.

Are you a skydiver? Or would you just like to feel like one? Wind tunnels are a *blast*! They create a column of wind so you feel like you're whooshing through the air. But if you're already a pro, consider joining Jump for the Cause. It's a semiannual event of expert women skydivers who jump in formation to raise money for breast cancer research at the City of Hope.

If you prefer, however, that your plane land before you step out of it, you can still help by donating to Jump for the Cause, Inc., 886 S. Los Robles Avenue, Pasadena, CA 91106 or www.JumpfortheCause.com.

Since its inception in 1999, Jump for the Cause has raised more than $1 million. The event takes place every few years at Perris Valley Skydiving, in Perris, California. In 2005, the event set a new world record: 151 women jumped in formation, joining hands in midair to create a giant flower in the sky.

Debbie Tenzer

Skydivers, ages twenty-one to sixty-two, came from fifteen countries and included three cancer survivors. All of the women were experts who had competed many times before. Some had traveled to competitive events for a year in advance to practice.

On the day of the event, twenty-three women boarded each airplane, and their seven planes flew in birdlike formation at 100 miles per hour. The altitude of the jump was 17,000 feet, and participants began taking oxygen at 15,000 feet.

Skydiver Melanie Peschio said, "When you jump, it doesn't feel like you're falling at all. You're moving—*flying*—and you're in control. You know that you have to give 100 percent to do your job, and the significance of why we were jumping that day made us work harder.

"We were a determined group of women, very passionate about helping women with cancer, and we really got to know one another. A lot of planning, choreography, and heart went into it—a serious time commitment. But it was a big honor to participate."

The average jump from leap to landing lasted three to five minutes. A woman is diagnosed with breast cancer every three minutes.

Do One Nice Thing

With a Song in Your Heart

Do you sing or play a musical instrument? If so, seniors in a residential care facility will delight in your music. Go see them. Your visit will be a welcome respite from their daily routine, and your energy will enliven their day. You don't need a great voice— just a big heart.

Take your children and well-behaved dog or cat with you too. The residents will enjoy giving affection to your pet.

Music touches us in a way that nothing else does. There's evidence that patients who are unresponsive due to a stroke or dementia are still able to feel music and be stimulated by it.

••••••••••••••••••••••••

When my sister and I were nine and ten, we used to play our guitars and sing folk songs on Sundays at the retirement home where our grandmothers lived. We weren't particularly talented, but our audience

Debbie Tenzer

wasn't picky, and many of them would clap and sing along with us. However, some residents seemed lost in their own worlds; they were suffering from Parkinson's or Alzheimer's disease, and didn't hear us at all. Or so we thought.

One day when we finished our songs, I noticed that one of the nurses was wiping tears from her eyes. I asked her what was wrong. She pointed to an elderly lady propped up awkwardly in a chair and said, "Minnie has barely moved as long as I've been here—three years at least. She doesn't talk and doesn't react at all. But when you were singing, she was nodding her head in time to the music and moving her lips. Not a lot, but she was doing it. She was happy! If I hadn't seen it, I wouldn't believe it."

· ·

"Sixty percent of nursing home residents receive no visitors. So don't underestimate the impact that one smile, one moment of laughter, and the other gifts of human presence can have on the lives of individuals who are now relying on others for their daily quality of life."—Mary, advocate for the elderly in Ohio

Do One Nice Thing

The Beat Goes On

You can save a life—actually up to eight lives. Sign up online to be an organ and tissue donor. It takes just a few minutes. Someone's organ donation could save your life, or the life of someone you love. Visit www.DonateLife.net.

"What's it like to accept a kidney? It was the most extreme case of mixed feelings I've ever had. On the one hand, a live donor would save my life, and release me from dialysis and its risks—truly a miracle.

"On the other hand, there was guilt over the idea that someone had to go through the risk of laparoscopic surgery for me to live. What if something happened? Or what if they had an accident later and needed a kidney? Then there was the extreme humbling of self required to accept a gift I had no way of repaying. Ever. A gift beyond any scope I could imagine, and it had to be given, and accepted, without any thought of recompense. There was a purity in this that was difficult to bear.

"Now, nearly five years later, I feel continuously

Debbie Tenzer

grateful and in constant awe that someone gave me a part of their body so I could live. I think the world of my donor, and so do those who know the story. It's bonded us in a way few people get to experience."—Laura

Do One Nice Thing

Pink-Link

**Click to donate free mammograms
for women who can't afford them
at www.TheBreastCancerSite.com.**

Vicki Tashman founded Pink-Link, a central online database of breast cancer survivors and patients everywhere. Most people who complete cancer treatment want to get as far away from it as possible, and it's understandable, but Vicki did the opposite—she rushed toward it in order to help other women. She says, "I was very blessed to have had a lot of love and support throughout my treatment, but I met women who didn't."

So Vicki created the database where survivors can input details about their cancers and treatments. Newly diagnosed women can search the database and learn, and they can do it right in the comfort of their homes. Plus, the mentor-patient relationship makes treatment more tolerable.

If you, a colleague, or someone you love has breast cancer, visit www.Pink-Link.org.

Debbie Tenzer

Take One Every Day

Donate vitamins online for low-income children, pregnant mothers, members of the National Guard, and the elderly at www.NourishAmerica.org.

"Malnourished children are angry children.... Any little thing would set them off."—Principal Bessie Gardner, Ruleville Elementary School, Mississippi

•••••••••••••••••••••••

They're not angry anymore. In fact, they're blossoming, thanks to Mary and Michael Morton, founders of Nourish America. Michael, a psychologist, was managing homeless shelters in Central California when an idea struck him. Why not give vitamins and protein bars to children living on the street? Maybe it would fortify them and protect them from illness. He tried it, and the results were so striking that he was asked to start a nonprofit vitamin program for homeless kids.

Today Nourish America provides daily vitamins and nourishing foods to tens of thousands of at-risk children at more than five hundred sites in all fifty states. It also provides daily multivitamins and calcium to low-income pregnant women, members of the

Do One Nice Thing

National Guard, and seniors across the United States. Mary and Michael find out who needs help, then get manufacturers to ship vitamins directly to agencies and schools.

Every spring, Mary and Michael survey the effects of vitamins on the people taking them. One success story is stunning: Ruleville Elementary School of Ruleville, Mississippi, was placed on probation by the state for low test scores. The students were malnourished, poor, and most had behavioral problems. All day long Ms. Gardner and her staff were dealing with discipline problems. Suspecting malnourishment was the cause, she approached the Mortons for help. The school was granted a supply of chewable multivitamin/minerals for the children. Each school day before lunch, the school staff distributed vitamins to the students. Bottles of vitamins were also given to parents so children could take vitamins at home.

"The parents who didn't want to comply, I challenged them," said Ms. Gardner. "I told them to take the vitamins themselves—just double the dose—and they'd see for themselves how much good these vitamins can do."

Mary said parents were convinced when they saw *their own behavior* improve. People who worked night shifts reported that they had more energy and stopped falling asleep at work. Children's behavior improved too, as did their self-esteem and overall health. After three years of taking vitamins, students at Ruleville are no longer on probation. Thanks to Mary and Michael Morton, tens of thousands of kids have turned their lives around and are looking forward to a brighter future.

Do One Nice Thing

Dinner Tree

Organize a "dinner tree," a "school lunch tree," a "laundry tree," and a "carpool tree" for a sick friend. Ask a few friends to commit to bringing meals, packing lunches, washing the family's clothes, and driving the kids for one day each week until your friend has recovered.

Some people who are used to being self-sufficient and in control automatically refuse help when they face a crisis. It doesn't occur to them that they need help because they are so accustomed to helping others. Even if they turn down your offer, persist—especially if you're providing food.

························

"During the school year, the husband of my son's teacher was diagnosed with bladder cancer. Of course she was very upset. I offered to prepare some dinners for her, but she refused. I did it anyway.

"She was so grateful and so appreciative and hadn't realized how much the meals would help

Debbie Tenzer

out her and her family. I then organized members of the school community to bring meals to her every other day for three months. I continued to make a meal for her each week throughout that time."
—Susan

Do One Nice Thing

5

Do One Nice Thing in Town

Our towns and cities are extensions of our homes, and the people we see every day can be like family to us. For example,

→ the mail carrier who greets us by name

→ the waitress who says, "What can I get for you, hon?"

→ the hairdresser or barber who listens and empathizes

→ the police officers and firefighters who are there when we need them

→ the neighbor whose kindness we can depend on

Some people complain: "People move around so much." "We don't even know our neighbors." "These days it's hard to feel connected to each other."

Well, some things are hard, and some things are not:

→ Getting to know every new neighbor is hard. But inviting *one* neighbor over for coffee is not.

→ Reducing rush-hour traffic is hard. But refraining from blasting your horn is not.

→ Feeding every hungry person is hard. But paying for a stranger's burger is not.

→ Making the world a more compassionate place is hard. But smiling at someone is not.

Here are some personal ways that you can make life brighter, kinder, and friendlier in your town.

Debbie Tenzer

Smile

Smile at people. It might not seem like much. But think of it this way: You might be the only bright thing they see that day.

Sometimes when I'm being interviewed on the radio, I ask listeners to call in and tell me about the nice things strangers have done for them, or that they have done for strangers.

One man told me that he used to walk a long way to work each day—until a stranger surprised him by pulling his truck over to the side of the road and giving him a bicycle. Wow!

Another man explained how proud he felt when his daughter wanted to give her books to a needy child in her class. He figured out how to do it anonymously, so the girl's family wouldn't feel embarrassed. What a beautiful message he communicated to his daughter! It's not only what you give but *how* you give it that counts.

Then a woman called and said, "I make a point of smiling at everyone." In contrast to what the other people did, I thought smiling is skating on *thin nice.* But then I thought, no, smiling is truly a nice thing to

Do One Nice Thing

do. Imagine how sad life would be if every face we saw wore a frown.

"If you don't have enough things or money to share, a smile is a lovely gift. It doesn't matter that we are Muslims or Christians or Jews or Hindus or belong to any other faith. We can all smile and make this world like heaven."—Imran

Debbie Tenzer

I'm a Beautician, Not a Magician*

Believe me, my beautician really is a magician! Surprise yours with a thank-you note.

Most women I know have very affectionate relationships with their hairdressers. We can never thank them enough for making us look and feel better. They are not only highly skilled professionals but also our confidants. We love them because they are among the most caring, attentive listeners in our lives. Plus, thanks to Ricardo, my husband thinks I still have the same hair color he married.

Men and women see their barber or hairdresser regularly, but often don't even visit their doctor annually. Minorities in particular don't obtain adequate health care or information. Sadly, the result is a disproportionate amount of illness and death that could have been prevented.

In 1992, two months before his death from AIDS, tennis star Arthur Ashe founded the Arthur Ashe Institute for Urban Health (AAIUH). The purpose was to

*A sign in a Beverly Hills salon.

Do One Nice Thing

empower minorities to learn more about health issues and obtain better health care. The keys to achieving this? Hairdressers and barbers.

Drawing on the trusted relationships that they have with their clients, selected beauty professionals in urban areas are being educated on health issues. Salons distribute health-related brochures and show videos on diabetes, asthma, menopause, cancer, heart disease, high blood pressure, and sexually transmitted diseases. Hairdressers and barbers are able to discuss these issues with their clients and encourage them to get help (www.ArthurAsheInstitute.org).

Debbie Tenzer

9-1-1 Munchies

**Thank the members of your police
and fire department by delivering
some goodies to them.**

Karyn Gross from Encino, California, is a much beloved
gynecologist. Every evening after work she makes a
few stops on her way home. Her first stop is a local
cafe, where she picks up a bag of pastries from the
friendly baristas who are expecting her. Her second
stop is the Los Angeles Police Department, where she
drops off some of those same goodies for police officers. Her third stop is the Los Angeles Fire Department, where she drops off the rest.

   This daily ritual is one of the ways Dr. Gross ex-
presses her gratitude to the police and firefighters in
her city. She's also been known to bring them the occasional long Subway sandwich, and for many years
she gave flu shots to the firefighters, prompting one
(male) firefighter to say, "Excuse me. I have to visit
my gynecologist."

9-1-1 and 9/11 are inextricably linked in the minds
of most Americans. Emergency responders lost their

Do One Nice Thing

lives in horrific numbers as they rushed to evacuate victims on that terrible day. Search and Rescue crews from fire departments around the United States went to New York to search through the rubble of the World Trade Center. They felt honor-bound to this work in memory of the victims and their colleagues who perished.

Since then, September 11 has become unofficial Firefighter Appreciation Day. People make pilgrimages to their local fire stations bearing flowers and candles, wanting to express gratitude and solidarity but not knowing how else to do it. Firefighters appreciate the attention, and here are some other ways you can thank them: Donate cooking utensils, exercise equipment, or bedding. Egg-crate–type mattress toppers are especially appreciated because they make older mattresses much more comfortable. Gifts of food are often appreciated too.

When you make an offer, be prepared to be rebuffed—at first. If you ask firefighters how you can help them, they'll most likely say, "Thank you, but we don't need anything." But if you tell them that you *happen to have* some extra almost-new cookware or a slightly used treadmill you're trying to give away . . . their eyes might light up.

Debbie Tenzer

Land of the Free

On Election Day, drive someone to the polls who needs a lift. If you don't know anyone who needs a ride, contact your political party's local office.

Do you always vote? I know some people who do. They are immigrants to the United States from the former Soviet Union, and I taught English to them.

One class member, Boris, was an eternal optimist, always smiling. Surprisingly, one day he slumped into class looking dejected. He haltingly explained that a woman "in small clothes" (a skimpy outfit) bumped into him on a bus, and the next thing he knew his wallet was gone. His whole life was in his wallet—his meager savings as well as irreplaceable documents and photos.

I told him, "We need to report it to the police." He was aghast. No one in his country would call the police to report a stolen wallet. The police there would expect to be paid a bribe, so the victim would get robbed twice. I told him, "Don't worry. This is how we do it."

Do One Nice Thing

As curious students gathered around, I made the call. The Los Angeles police officer was very polite and patiently took a report over the phone: "What was the wallet's value?" Boris: "Very expensive! Twenty dollars!" And so it went. The police officer told him that he knew it felt terrible to have one's wallet stolen, but frankly the chances were not high of recovering the wallet. The officer thanked him for filing a report. Boris felt better. He had been treated with respect, and his loss had been acknowledged.

A month later Boris rushed over to me full of excitement. "Look!" He held out a manila envelope stamped: "PROPERTY DISCARDED IN U.S. MAILBOX." The thief had grabbed the cash, tossed the rest into a mailbox, and incredibly Boris had received his wallet back with all his documents and photos. He was euphoric. Beaming, he told me, "I love America. Even the thieves have a heart!"

Not really, but why argue? Boris was determined to find the silver lining in a cloud, and he found it. And if he could find it with everything he had been through in his life, I could find it too. Maybe we natives understand the reality of America better than my students did. But they understand the reason for America in a way that we don't. They're grateful to their adopted country, and they *always* vote.

Debbie Tenzer

"The Constitution only gives people the right to pursue happiness. You have to catch it yourself."
—Benjamin Franklin

Do One Nice Thing

I'm from the Government. I'm Here to Help You. Really!

Sometimes we take for granted the many dedicated and kind government employees who are doing a great job.

Write a note to your mayor or governor to compliment your police, fire department, schools, library, sanitation services, transportation department, and others.

"I was driving from Norfolk, Virginia, where I was stationed in the Navy, to my parents' home in Rhode Island. I had plenty of gas in the car and a gas credit card, but didn't have fifteen cents for the Old Saybrook toll on the Connecticut Turnpike.

"I parked at the side of the road and looked at my maps for a legal way to go around the toll booth. A police officer walked up to my window and asked why I was sitting there. I explained my predicament, and

Debbie Tenzer

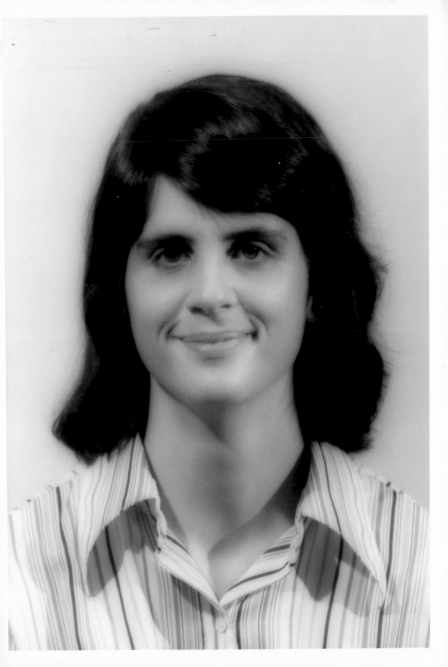

PHOTO CREDIT:

Annie Caroline Butt
Charleston, S. C.
803-577-0547

without hesitating, he reached into his pocket and handed me a $5 bill. 'Go on home, kid.' I was dumbfounded! He refused to give me his name so I could repay him when I got home. So, for the record, thank you, Officer."—Willy

Do One Nice Thing

I've Got Your Back

Do you know your neighbors? If you do, you're fortunate. If you don't, invite yours over for coffee. Get to know one another, and share information about what's going on in the neighborhood. It's comforting to know who's nearby. Who knows? Someday you might need each other.

"In 1976 my husband had a heart attack in the spring, and one neighbor in particular came and got our farm ground ready for planting. Naturally, we were very appreciative, and my husband was able to help other farmers in years to come.

"Then in 2005 the farmer that had helped us fell and broke a hip. So our son and my husband were able to go and help a group harvest his crops—twenty-nine years after he had helped us. Farmer helping farmer is a way of life for us."—Mary Ann

• •

"When I was first married and very young, we moved to Alaska. I didn't know anyone. A kind lady brought me over a loaf of banana nut bread that she had made. I never forgot it."—Pat

Debbie Tenzer

Wave Them In

Stuck in traffic? Be gracious to someone by pausing for a moment and allowing them to drive into your lane or walk across the street.

Rush hour is a tough time to be nice. Blaring horns and screeching brakes can make anyone a bit tense. Let's face it: It's hard to feel generous in bumper-to-bumper traffic.

But one night I learned a lesson from a driver in front of me. With a wave of her hand, she signaled to a waiting car in a parking lot: "Come on in!" The grateful driver, who'd been idling awhile, excitedly waved back to her and drove forward.

Suddenly I snapped out of my *en garde* mind-set. I waved in the next waiting car and received a nice thank-you wave in return. It felt good. The driver behind me waved someone in too.

Try it the next time you're stuck in traffic. You might start a nice chain reaction.

• • • • • • • • • • • • • • • •

"My girlfriend and I were in Boston for three days, and it seemed that *everyone* was doing nice things for us. When we got on the subway, a young man gave

Do One Nice Thing

up his seat and politely told us to sit down. Wow! Every time we looked at the map someone stopped to help us. One man was going the same way we were and took us with him to make sure we didn't get lost.

"Cars would stop for us when we weren't even ready to cross the street. They would just wait for us! The hot dog vendor even cut our hot dog in half so we could split it. I know these are little things, but it made our trip a lot nicer."—Becky

Debbie Tenzer

Barrier Busters

Take a look around your town. Let shop owners know when entries or aisles are difficult for disabled people to navigate. Sometimes all that's needed is to install a short ramp next to steps, or to move a display over a few inches, to enable disabled people to come in and enjoy a shopping experience.

One out of every five people in the United States—more than 54 million people—identify themselves as disabled. Despite laws to afford them equal access, disabled people still find many buildings difficult to enter.

Vince Staskel is a paralegal in New York who protects the rights of people with disabilities. He uses a wheelchair, and he created a program that he calls "Barrier Busters"—teaching volunteers how to politely inform businesses about the needs of the disabled.

He said, "There were many times when my wife and I could not enter older stores. We slowed down to look at them—especially some charming antiques shops—but they had steps without ramps. We saw that we couldn't go in so we just drove by."

Do One Nice Thing

"Actually, it costs about $200 for a business to install a ramp over a couple of steps so disabled people can enter. The business would easily increase its patronage and earn back that money many times over. I think most business owners would be happy to accommodate us if they were aware of the problem."

Promoting justice is a gratifying career, but actually it's not the one Vince dreamed of when he was in school. He wanted to pursue a career in the performing arts, but since he used a wheelchair and there was little wheelchair accessibility in the 1970s, especially in broadcasting studios, sound booths, and stages, he couldn't do so. Even worse, his classmates and instructors patronized and discouraged him.

But Vince is a determined man. He held on to his dream, and now it's coming true. He is cofounding With-TV (www.with-tv.com), a cable television channel that showcases the creativity of performers we seldom see on television—people with disabilities. Thanks to Vince and his colleagues, soon disabled people will not be invisible on television anymore.

Debbie Tenzer

Just Say WHOA

Don't pass along a bad mood.
Don't catch it in the first place.

Some people are simply not nice. They holler. They honk. They push around everyone in their way. Unfortunately, crabbiness is not a victimless crime. When mean people bark at us, we often turn around and bark at other people.

Instead of acting like a victim, do something nice for yourself. Here's a simple method I learned to remove the bad guy or gal's power over you, and stop a mean spree in its tracks.

Example: A man in a speeding car cuts you off in traffic, then screams a vile obscenity *at you* even though *he* almost caused an accident.

Instead of freezing in fear or yelling back, imagine the perpetrator as a screaming toddler: *WHOA! He's wearing nothing but a diaper! Now in full tantrum mode, he's shrieking at the top of his lungs, turning red in the face, pumping his tiny fists in the air and kicking his chubby little legs. Wow, is he mad! But now he's no longer sitting in his hot muscle car screaming at you. He's in a crib, where he deserves to be, behind bars.*

Case closed.

Do One Nice Thing

The Cookie Man

Make Mondays sweeter. Carry a package of cookies with you and hand them out at your office or wherever you go. (It's also a fantastic way to make friends with fellow passengers on an airplane, bus, or train.)

When retiree Bob Mortensen takes his daily stroll, everyone smiles. This is because Bob makes a habit of carrying cookies with him, and he gives them out to everyone working outdoors in his Southern California neighborhood. Even people who don't know Bob personally, such as the gardeners and restaurant workers, call out "Cookie Man!" when they see him. He's the most popular guy in town.

. . . .

"When I was sixteen, Bob gave me a cookie. Diamonds came later!"—Betty, Bob's wife for more than sixty years

Debbie Tenzer

Hear a Siren,
Say a Prayer

What if the next time an ambulance sped by with its siren screaming, you said a little prayer?

What if everyone who heard the siren said one?

What if you were the patient in the ambulance, terribly frightened. But then you realized that everyone nearby is praying for you. Wouldn't it make you feel a lot better?

On a visit to Jerusalem years ago, I was riding in a city bus across town on a Saturday night. I noticed how different it was from riding a bus at home, where people were quiet and kept to themselves. In Jerusalem loads of exuberant young people clambered on at every stop, and they chatted over the sounds of blaring Israeli pop music.

The party was in full swing when the bus suddenly came to a halt. Someone said there was a car accident ahead. The bus driver descended from the

Do One Nice Thing

bus, and for several minutes no one knew what was going on. Then the driver returned. But this time he was accompanied by three men, and they were carrying an injured man.

Passengers immediately moved to make room as the men carefully laid the victim on the floor and comforted him. The driver jumped back into his seat, cranked the ignition, and floored the accelerator. Our bus had become an ambulance speeding to Hadassah Medical Center. The laughter and music had vanished and, except for the soft moans of the injured man and occasional grinding of the bus, there was silence. I had the feeling that everyone was praying. I know I was.

Debbie Tenzer

Want a Lift?

Do you see the same people day after day walking long distances to and from work, or waiting for a long time for a bus or train? Can you offer someone a ride?

"Recently my wife was in hospital here in Cambridgeshire, England, and I was there to see her every day. You get to see the same old faces waiting for the hospital transport or a cab to take them home.

"So after visiting my wife, I went to the waiting area and asked if anyone wanted a lift on route to where I live. People looked at me suspiciously, and I knew what they were thinking: 'What's the catch? How much? Is he for real?'

"I said, 'No catch—the offer is there. I have spare seats in the car, and I'm leaving now. Or you can wait in the cold for an hour-plus for the hospital transport—your choice.'

"I took three folks home right to their front doors and explained on the way why I was doing it—to spread the word about doing a nice thing. I said, 'Try it yourself in some small way.' They all thought it was a nice idea and would give it a go.

Do One Nice Thing

"It is very difficult for some folks to accept some-thing for nothing, or just accept an offer of help with-out accusing someone of being on the make. It says a lot about the way we are untrusting and on the watch all the time."—Guy

● ●

Yes, but in one day Guy changed the minds of three people, and maybe they'll pass his nice thing along.

Debbie Tenzer

Ahead of Time

**When you're walking down the
street, keep an eye on the parking
meters. If you see that a meter is
about to expire, insert a coin.
Imagine how delighted the driver
will be *not* to get a ticket.**

When I started Do One Nice Thing, this was one of
the first nice things I did. In Los Angeles, the parking
enforcement officers told me that it's illegal to put a
coin in an already-expired parking meter, unless it's
for your own car.

So I only insert coins in meters with a couple of
minutes left. Then, like an elf, I vanish. Maybe the
car's owner won't even realize that the meter ran out
of time. On the other hand, maybe she or he will wonder, "What nice person did that for me?" and they'll
do it for someone else.

Do One Nice Thing

How's It Going?

Reach out to someone. You never know what might happen.

"I was at the checkout stand completing my weekly family shopping. The cashier was a charming young Vietnamese woman. I complimented her on her English. She shared that she wanted to learn more in order to make a better life for her family. I pulled out my business card and wrote the number for BEACON, a literacy program of the Benedictine Sisters of Virginia that pairs a volunteer tutor with an adult learner.

"A year later out of the blue, she called me! She had found my card and wanted to thank me for my words of encouragement. She had earned her GED and enrolled at the community college. A small act of kindness on my part was rewarded by the opportunity to share her sense of accomplishment."—Christine

. . . .

"My husband, Manny, and I were taking our morning walk, when we passed a woman walking a dog. Manny said, 'Good morning,' to her. She looked shocked, hesitated, then replied, 'Good morning.'

"Then Manny ran ahead of me (I walk a tad slow for him) and she came up to me and asked, 'Is that your

Debbie Tenzer

husband?' I said yes, and she said, 'I just have to tell you how nice it was that he said hello to me. I've lived in this neighborhood a long time and no one's ever done that. Please tell him how much I appreciate it.' Who knew how much a 'Good morning' could mean?"—Judi

Do One Nice Thing

HELLO!
My Name Is . . .

Try wearing a name tag for a day.

Did you ever attend a meeting where you needed to wear one of those adhesive name labels and forget to remove it afterward? I did and went about my business in town.

A wonderful thing happened. People who didn't know me called me by my name. "Excuse me, Debbie, do you happen to know what time it is?" People were much friendlier than usual, which gave me the opportunity to ask them what their names were too.

I liked it so much that sometimes I wear a "HELLO! My Name Is Debbie" label just for fun. Does that sound weird? Try it. You might be pleasantly surprised.

Debbie Tenzer

Our Disposals Eat Better Than People Do

Ask the manager of your favorite restaurant to donate its leftovers to a local food bank. If we could recover just 5 percent of the food wasted this year in the United States, we could feed about fourteen million people.

Many food and grocery companies don't realize that they can donate surplus, distressed, and damaged food. They are protected from liability when they donate in good faith to a nonprofit organization to benefit needy people.

Jim Fisk is a local grocer in Sharon, Vermont, who accepts returns from a bread/cake distributor and sends them to two food banks in his area. He also keeps a jar on his store's counter for customers to drop in their change, adding up to more than $50 each month to donate to the hungry. He says, "It does go a long way, and we are so pleased that we can give back to the community and to those less fortunate."

When you're shopping for groceries, buy a couple extra cans of soup or tuna and donate them to your

Do One Nice Thing

local food bank. Many local houses of worship and schools have collection bins. How about starting your own collection at work every Monday? Here are more ways to help:

••••••••••••••••••••••••

"One evening we were at a Steak n Shake and a man sat in the booth across from ours. I overheard him questioning the waitress about the prices for each item, obviously concerned about the cost. His clothing was dirty and he looked tired. When we went to the counter to pay our bill, I paid for his at the same time. I asked the cashier to wait until we left, then let the man know that his meal was covered. How simple it was to help, and what a wonderful feeling I had inside!"—Karen

••••••••••••••••••••••••

"I keep fresh fruit in my car. Whenever I see homeless people I share it with them."—Lori

••••••••••••••••••••••••

More information on how food companies can help is available through Feeding America (www .FeedingAmerica.org).

Debbie Tenzer

Well Done!

**Leave a big tip and little note for a
wonderful waiter. You can also do
this at other businesses, including
hotels, retail stores, and for
repairmen who come to your
house. Or ask to speak to the
employee's manager to praise
the person who has been
exceptionally kind or helpful.
Track down people's bosses and
write them letters and e-mails
praising them for having the
wisdom to hire such fantastic staff.**

"Sometimes we have to reach out to pay a deserved
compliment. In a restaurant we say to the server,
'Please have the chef come to our table.' When she or
he arrives, I say, 'When my wife says twice that her
meal is delicious, the chef should hear it directly.'
When the meal is over, we ask to see the manager. We
compliment him or her for the fine dinners and service. You should see the changed expression on all of
these individuals' faces who are more accustomed to
being called on the carpet for what's wrong."—Bob

Do One Nice Thing

Be My Guest

Pay for the person behind you:

➜ **at the drive-through restaurant**

➜ **on the bridge or toll road**

➜ **on the bus or in line for coffee**

"I was on my way home from work, waiting in line at the Tacony-Palmyra Bridge to pay my toll. As I approached the booth, the clerk said that the car ahead of me had paid my $2 toll. How nice! To the lady in the metallic blue car, thank you. She inspired me to do something nice for someone else."—Taryn

· ·

"While I was over at a Dairy Queen with my sister, I was up to get a glass of water when I saw the cashier getting an order. I told the cashier that I would pay for that order. He and his co-workers' jaws dropped. I didn't know what the customer thought but I felt happy to help."—Maria

Debbie Tenzer

They Deliver

Where would we be without our dedicated letter carriers? Say "thank you" by leaving a snack and note for yours.

All my neighbors look forward to seeing Ray Peoples, our letter carrier. It's not unusual to see people handing him sodas, muffins, and other treats. Why? He always has an infectious smile, a warm greeting, and a wave for everyone, and he knows all of us by name.

One day when I was driving my daughter home from school, we passed by a birthday party at one of our neighbor's homes. We slowed down to look at the colorful balloons and cute preschool-age guests. Suddenly my daughter shouted, "There's Ray!" Sure enough, someone had grabbed him to pose for a photo with the little birthday girl. She was holding his hand. Then as he waved good-bye to return to his route, her mother handed him a plate with a slice of layer cake—a snack for the road.

Do One Nice Thing

6

Do One Nice Thing Around the Globe

"The whole world is a very narrow bridge. The main thing is don't be afraid."—Rabbi Nachman of Breslov

I f I asked you to cross a street and stay within the crosswalk, you could easily do it. You do it all the time without giving it a second thought.

Now imagine the crosswalk is elevated 100 feet above the ground. The path is exactly the same size as it was when you crossed it thousands of times before. But suddenly it's not a crosswalk anymore: It's a bridge. Not a giant steel bridge like the Golden Gate, but a wobbly wooden one that sways and bobs under every step. Would you be afraid that you might fall? I would.

I'd think, *It's crowded! Who are all these people? What if someone pushes me, or loses his balance and accidentally knocks me over the edge? Or, what if the bridge's moorings rip loose? It could happen— sometimes bridges collapse. I wish I could see over the heads in front of me. I can't tell where I'm going. I'm scared.*

Well, in life we don't know exactly where we're going, but it doesn't have to scare us. Instead, we can reel in our anxiety and extend a hand to our fellow travelers. This chapter will show you how to assist people across the country and around the world, from homeless adults in Michigan to genocide survivors in Rwanda to a group of mothers who launched a small business in Bolivia.

Regardless of where we're from, we are one community on that narrow bridge. And wherever it leads, we're going there together. We have the power to make the journey safe and joyful for all of us—as long as we're not afraid.

Debbie Tenzer

Compassionate Banking

Help someone in a developing country lift themselves out of poverty. You can do it by making a "micro-loan" of just $25 or more through a fantastic nonprofit organization called Kiva (www.Kiva.org).

With your loan—and it is a loan, not a gift—you can be a compassionate "banker" and help someone launch a business. When your Kiva loan is repaid, you can choose to withdraw your funds or lend them to a new entrepreneur.

I'm a Kiva lender. It took just $25 and five minutes for me to support the clothing business of the Virgen del Socavón association of El Alto, Bolivia. The group consists of twenty women, most of whom are married with school-aged children, who sew athletic suits for the La Paz markets or schools. The women need capital to buy better-quality fabric and to improve their business, so they can provide their children with a better life.

Do One Nice Thing

My fellow lenders on this project are located across the globe—in the United States, Europe, Australia, and Japan. We are all strangers, but together we are extending a hand to a determined group of mothers in Bolivia.

Debbie Tenzer

Two Cents a Meal

Every time you eat, put a few cents (or more) into a little jar. Or on Monday, forego a coffee or a meal out, and instead donate the money to your local food bank, Heifer International, or Feeding America to help end hunger (www.heifer.org or www.feedingamerica.org).

The children at West Alexandria Church of the Brethren in Ohio are working to end hunger, one meal at a time. Their project is called "2 Cents a Meal."

Children are reminded to contribute a little at every meal throughout the week, and are given a label to put on their tin can or other container to collect their coins.

On Sunday at church, the children come forward and deposit their coins in a large jar. The money is donated to the Heifer International project. The money helps buy livestock for developing countries, so needy villages can become self-sustaining and the villagers won't be hungry anymore.

Do One Nice Thing

More Ways to Help

Play the Free Rice game at www.FreeRice.com. For every word you get right, advertisers donate rice to the United Nations World Food Program to feed hungry people in developing countries.

Click www.TheHungerSite.com daily to donate free food.

Debbie Tenzer

Would You Like to Buy a Goat?

**Donate a goat for $30 or
participate in other projects that
aid people in developing countries
at www.BearsWithoutBorders.org.**

In honor of their wedding, Nice-o-holic newlyweds
Aviva Presser and Erez Lieberman wanted to do something different. The two Harvard and MIT PhD students wanted to spread their joy.

So they founded a nonprofit organization and
named it Bears Without Borders in honor of their first
project, making teddy bears for needy children in
South Africa. Next Aviva and Erez launched a project
to purchase goats for families in Rwanda. Many families lost their heads-of-household during the 1994
genocide, when 800,000 people were killed in 100
days. AIDS is also taking a toll, and there are hundreds of thousands of orphans. But Rwandans are re-
building their lives.

A pair of goats is a fantastic gift for them. Able to
graze even on poor, dry land, goats supply several
quarts of milk per day—a wonderful source of nutrition for malnourished children. Extra milk and cheese

Do One Nice Thing

can be sold, providing additional income for families. Even goat manure is productive. It enriches the soil so farmers can raise crops for their families. To further the spirit of giving, the first kid born to a donated pair of goats is given away to another impoverished family.

•••••••••••••••••••••

"When you get in a tight place and everything goes against you, until it seems as if you could not hold on a minute longer, never give up then, for that is just the place and time when the tide will turn."—Harriet Beecher Stowe

Debbie Tenzer

The Rickshaw Puller

I think this is a special tale even though there's no "nice thing" for us to do. That's part of the story, however.

Swapan Adhikari is a rickshaw puller in Bidoypur, India. He lives in a tiny shanty with his wife and their two grown sons. Each week he saves a little money—not for himself, but to buy school books for needy children.

When he was young, he couldn't afford to go to school, so now he enables others. Eight years ago he began by buying books for seven poor boys, who were thrilled. Recently he gave books to 125 children.

He'd help more if his cow hadn't been stolen. He used to sell the milk so he could buy books. Now he pulls his rickshaw instead for an extra hour each day. It's hard, but he believes it's worth it.

My friends and I were very moved when we heard about Mr. Adhikari's kindness. E-mails started flying:

"That man deserves a new cow!"
"How can we get him a cow?"
"Is anyone going to India? I'll send some money to help him buy a cow."

Do One Nice Thing

It turned out that a new cow in India would cost about 1,000 rupees ($250), but Mr. Adhikari did not have a bank account. Even if he did, since September 11, 2001, Homeland Security regulations had been enacted to prevent terrorists from receiving money from the United States. Mr. Adhikari was certainly not a terrorist, but we had no way to send him money.

Instead I suggested that we send notebooks and school supplies to him for the students in his village. I wrote about this to Ravi Chandar in India, who originally told me about Mr. Adhikari. Ravi Chandar was grateful for the offer but did not want us to send school supplies. This time all I could do was send good wishes.

He responded, "Beloved Mother, thank you for your kind words. Your politeness and courtesy have really touched us. May God bless you all that are good and great. Love, Ravi."

Sometimes trying to help is all we can do.

Searching for Buried Treasure?

Support your favorite charity or school whenever you search the Internet at www.GoodSearch.com. Choose a cause, then search on the Internet as you would using any search engine. GoodSearch donates to your cause every time you search.

Every time you search, GoodSearch will donate 1¢ to a charity you choose. If one thousand people with the same charity search twice a day for a year, the charity will earn $7,300—a *real* treasure.

Your favorite charities will also benefit when you shop at www.GoodShop.com. Just choose your cause and go shopping at any of the five hundred online stores affiliated with GoodShop. Up to 30 percent of your purchase will be donated to the charity of your choice.

What are your favorite causes? Write them down. Then the next time you search the Internet, choose one of them as your GoodSearch beneficiary.

Do One Nice Thing

Priceless Lessons

**Create a priceless gift: Interview
an elderly person about his or her
life. Make a video or little book
and give it to them. Save a copy
for yourself too.**

Do young people take freedom for granted? George Ciampa thinks so: "Young people need to know that freedom is more than being able to stay out all night."

The World War II veteran led a group of high school teachers and a documentary film crew to Belgium, where they met with survivors of the Nazi occupation. George, eighty-three, raised all the funds himself. He also brought along two fellow veterans, and they spoke with Belgian children while there.

The goal: to transmit to young people what losing your freedom means. George remembers. When he was eighteen, the Californian landed on a Normandy beach on D-day, June 6, 1944. Assigned to the 607th Graves Registration Company, he searched for soldiers' bodies and prepared them for burial.

During the Battle of the Bulge, the bloodiest battle of the war in Europe, George's company bivouacked in the Belgian woods. It was the coldest winter in thirty

Debbie Tenzer

years. His company gathered the dead on the frozen battlefields and buried them at the Henri-Chapelle American cemetery nearby.

After the war, George returned home, resumed his life, and a different kind of freedom was on his mind: college and girls. Later he was busy with work (he was a salesman) and family. Widowed young, he raised two children by himself. The war was in the past. But in 1994, urged by his kids and his fiancée (now his wife, Dottie), he returned to Europe for the fiftieth anniversary of D-day.

He looked up two acquaintances in Belgium he had known during the war who lived near the Henri-Chapelle cemetery. They welcomed him with open arms, and their meeting became the first of many. That's when George decided he needed to tell as many young people as possible about the importance of freedom.

He produced two documentaries about his trip to Belgium and a subsequent trip to Normandy, *Let Freedom Ring: The Lesson Is Priceless* and *Let Freedom Ring: Memories from France.* They have been shown in schools. George wants to spread the message to as many young people as possible. There's no time to waste. One of the veterans who accompanied George on the trip passed away the day after filming was completed.

Do One Nice Thing

"It is nice to know that the people of Belgium are so appreciative and welcomed Mr. Ciampa. My dad, Jack Ritchie, 101st Airborne, now deceased, fought at the Battle of the Bulge, and I feel Mr. Ciampa's film is an honor to his memory too."—Pam

Debbie Tenzer

Soles4Souls

Send a pair of new or gently used shoes, any style and any size, for people who truly need them. Mail to Soles4Souls, Inc., 315 Airport Road, Roanoke, AL 36274

"One, two, buckle my shoe." Most of us remember that first line of the beloved nursery rhyme we learned when we were little. Shoes: we take them for granted. But more than 300 million children worldwide have never owned a single pair of shoes.

When we choose a new pair of shoes, we usually think about style and fit. But for people who have no shoes, they simply want to protect their feet from injuries. A pair of shoes can actually save a life.

Soles4Souls ships donated shoes from North America to people who need them all over the world. Founded by Wayne Esley, a footwear industry executive, the organization contributed more than 1 million pairs of shoes to victims of the Asian tsunami and Hurricanes Katrina and Rita, and it continues to send shoes to people in crisis.

Some of the people helped by Soles4Souls include:

Do One Nice Thing

- → women in villages who walk as much as 10 miles, barefoot, to bring water to their families every day
- → women and children in domestic abuse shelters who have fled their homes in a hurry, without any belongings
- → students in Appalachia who don't have shoes to wear to school
- → poor men and women around the world who sort through landfills for goods on which to survive

....

"The excellence of a gift lies in its appropriateness rather than in its value."—Charles Dudley Warner

Debbie Tenzer

Clean Slate

When you travel, bring home small complimentary soaps, shampoos, and other toiletries. Homeless shelters will be grateful for them. You will help their guests maintain their dignity by feeling and looking better. Mail toiletries to your closest shelter or to Westside Food Bank, 1710 22nd Street, Santa Monica, CA 90404.

A person who has been living on the streets gains tremendous self-esteem and self-confidence from the simple opportunity to shower, shave, brush their hair, and put on clean clothes.

John, a single dad with two young children, suffered a back injury and his life spun out of control. In quick order he lost his construction job, his health insurance, his savings, his home, and his kids. With no job prospects, he sent his children to live with a relative and he moved to the streets. In despair, he turned to alcohol and drugs.

Disheveled, dirty, and addicted, he was too ashamed to visit his children. Desperate for food, he found his

Do One Nice Thing

way to a homeless day center that provided meals. After receiving a hot meal, a caseworker offered him the opportunity to shower and get clean clothes. He was given a bag of travel-size toiletries, a razor, and clean clothes. He said, "When I looked in the mirror, I saw the man I used to be, and I became determined to find my way back to my old self."

With the help of the caseworker, he enrolled in a drug rehabilitation program and received the medical care he needed. His life got better. He became sober, moved into a transitional living shelter, and found a job as a site manager. Eventually he was able to get an apartment and bring his children to live with him again. "I am so grateful to the people who helped me. I almost lost everything, but they gave me hope, and now I have my life back, I have my kids back, and I am proud of who I am."

· ·

"The money I raise is helping to buy food for local hungry people, including over 42,000 children. As a single mom of three, there was a time when I needed help to feed my family, and I am so honored to help others in similar situations. No child should ever have to go without good nutrition, and I like being part of the solution."—Genevieve Riutort, director of Development at Westside Food Bank

Debbie Tenzer

More ways to help: Mail a box of breakfast bars, cereal, or macaroni and cheese to the Westside Food Bank (see introduction above) or a food bank near you.

Do One Nice Thing

Branch Out

**Send packets of flower seeds
for new families moving into
transitional housing units.**

*Growing a garden together improves the environment
and instills a sense of pride in one's home. A family's
outlook will be enhanced by the beauty of the flowers
and plants they raise.*

Mail to BARN, Sister Glenna Smith, OSB, 9541 Linton Hall Road, Bristow, VA 20136.

BARN is an exemplary transitional shelter for homeless women and their children, run by the Benedictine Sisters of Virginia. It rescues families facing imminent eviction or living in unsuitable circumstances, and gives them the support and skills they need to get back on their feet. People of all faiths are welcome.

Located on the verdant grounds of the St. Benedictine Monastery, the program provides housing and life-management skills to the moms and their kids, who spend eighteen to twenty-four months in the program, receiving the skills, help, and knowledge they need. Each mother is required to contribute 30

Debbie Tenzer

percent of her income to an escrow or savings account, which is returned to her in full when she leaves. For some mothers, it is the first savings account they've ever had.

The BARN program works. Its graduates have a phenomenal rate—96 percent—of maintaining permanent employment and living independently.

· ·

"Great trees grow from the smallest shoots; a terraced garden, from a pile of earth, and a journey of a thousand miles begins by taking the initial step."
—Lao-tzu

Do One Nice Thing

Warm Someone Up

Send gently used umbrellas, backpacks, hats, gloves, and scarves to Robert J. Delonis Center, 312 W. Huron Street, Ann Arbor, MI 48103.

In 1988, Lorraine Jara read an article that changed her life. Two young men had been boating near her town when their vessel capsized. Two women rescued them from the icy waters, but they had no radio or phone to call for help. The group tried to get the attention of other boaters and were noticed *but ignored*. When help finally arrived, it was too late. One of the young men had died.

The image of people being cold and disregarded stayed with Lorraine. How could people be so hard-hearted? Her frustration inspired her to create "Be Kind to Humankind Week," an annual event held August 25–31 that encourages people to help others with a different theme each day. It's been going strong for more than twenty years.

Lorraine is also a crusader for the Robert J. Delonis Center, her local homeless shelter. Homeless people have an especially rough time during the freezing

Debbie Tenzer

winter months. Every year Lorraine collects clothing donations for the shelter from all over town: local department stores, convention bureaus, senior centers, and her friends. She said, "There but for the grace of God go I. Anything is possible in today's uncertain world. But we can make it better when each of us shows kindness to others in small but powerful acts."

Do One Nice Thing

Become a
Recording Star

Can you donate a few hours to record textbooks? Contact Recording for the Blind & Dyslexic, National Headquarters, 20 Roszel Road, Princeton, NJ 08540, 866-RFBD-585/866-732-3585 (www.rfbd.org), which has branches throughout the United States.

Dr. Ellen Hocking-Keeler is a popular recording artist, but you won't hear her on the radio. She records *audio textbooks* for people with disabilities, and for eighteen years she has been a volunteer with Recording for the Blind & Dyslexic in Los Angeles.

RFB&D provides audio textbooks for students of all ages with vision, physical, and learning disabilities. The organization has thousands of volunteers recording audio textbooks in local recording studios. It is the world's largest producer of audio textbooks for people who can't effectively read standard print.

At eighty-one, Ellen has energy and acuity anyone would envy, and her specialty is recording upper-level math and statistics books. She used to record at

Debbie Tenzer

the Redondo Beach studio before becoming a "satellite" reader at home in a unique recording setup—in her bathroom. The small enclosed space is quiet, her very own recording "booth."

....

"I love books, and I started volunteering because I wanted to help give everybody, regardless of their abilities, the opportunity to love books too."—Rob, volunteer at Recording for the Blind & Dyslexic

Do One Nice Thing

Go Ahead, Make Their Day

**Compliment someone you admire.
If you can't tell them in person,
then call, write, or send an e-mail.
You're going to make someone
happy.**

Compliment . . .

→ a teacher who inspires you

→ a writer whose story moves you

→ a salesperson who is happy to help you

→ a member of the clergy whose sermon touches you

→ a leader who takes a stand you embrace

→ a doctor or nurse whose gentleness comforts you

Following a storm, a tree fell across our driveway. Actually, it wasn't just a tree, it was a *giant* eucalyptus tree—70 feet tall—and it barely missed falling on our house. If it had fallen just a few feet to the west, it would have crushed the roof of my little daughter's bed-

Debbie Tenzer

room as she slept. Miraculously no one was harmed and no serious damage was done.

The formerly majestic tree was lying "facedown" with its roots in the air. A city crew of a dozen men came over right away and began clearing away the thick trunk and long branches.

I noticed something interesting: Despite the cumbersome cranes, whining saws, and other heavy machinery they were operating, the burly men in heavy work boots carefully stepped around the flowers in our garden. How considerate of them!

I approached their supervisor and told him that I appreciated the men's special efforts. Over the roar of the machines, he shouted, "Don't thank me, thank *them*!" I did, and after writing down their names, I sent a letter to the mayor and the director of Street Services for the City of Los Angeles. As a result, each man received a special commendation in his personnel file.

Do One Nice Thing

Spring Break
Without a Hangover

Take a volunteer vacation.

Colleges and universities offer many community-service opportunities for their students and alumni. Additional opportunities are available for students and nonstudents through the following:

→ The Peace Corps (www.PeaceCorps.gov)

→ Habitat for Humanity (www.habitat.org)

→ Global Volunteers (www.GlobalVolunteers.org)

Take a guess: What do you think would cause thousands of eager college students to stand in a long line before dawn? The answer: an incredible vacation opportunity! That's not a shock, but where the vacations are might surprise you:

→ Harlem, New York, to work in a soup kitchen and homeless shelter

→ Tallahassee, Florida, to plant trees for the Nature Conservancy

→ the Louisiana Bayou, to work in a community center that assists Native Americans

Debbie Tenzer

➜ rural North Carolina, to care for children and
adults with developmental disabilities

When college students get a week off from school,
not all of them head to Cancún or Orlando. Instead of
spending Thanksgiving at home, students at James
Madison University (JMU) in Harrisonburg, Virginia,
paid $325 each and spent fifteen hours on a bus to
help with hurricane relief efforts in Biloxi, Mississippi.
Only fifty-six students were allowed on the trip, although many more requested to go. The JMU students and accompanying faculty were housed at a
local church and applied their muscles to removing
debris, assisting in construction efforts, and serving
meals at a shelter. They also exercised their hearts:
They listened, hugged, and bore witness to the survivors' generosity and courage. Students described
the trip as "life-changing."

Do One Nice Thing

7

Do One Nice Thing for Soldiers

What comes to mind when you think of "home"? Home is where the heart is. Home Sweet Home. HOME RUN! How about *homesick*?

No one yearns for home the way our soldiers* do, and we yearn for them too. No matter how old they are, we feel like they are our kids or our brothers and sisters; either way, they are far away and in danger.

And even though they've been taken out of America, no one can take America out of them. Wherever they go, they embody our values—kindness, generosity, freedom, and hope. Sadly, in many places, those

---

*Note: I use the word *soldiers* as an abbreviation for all the members of the United States Armed Forces: Army, Marine Corps, Navy, Air Force, and Coast Guard.

precious things are in short supply. Soldiers—past and present—say some of their best memories are of meeting local people around the world: getting acquainted with civilians, playing with their kids, and handing out chocolate bars.

Today a notebook and pencil are the new chocolate. Soldiers are fighting not only terrorism but also ignorance and illiteracy. Each year they give away hundreds of tons of school supplies, most sent by Americans at home.

Soldiers also hand out blankets, medicines, toys, diapers, and many other items. Besides fulfilling local families' personal needs, the gifts also increase bonds of trust between local people and our soldiers, enhancing their safety.

To our soldiers: thank you for your service.

To your families: thank you for your sacrifice.

Even though we're far from perfect, our country is magnificent. And there really is no place like home.

Here are some nice things you can do for service members, veterans, the men and women who come home wounded, and their families.

Debbie Tenzer

To Afghanistan with Love

Send school supplies to U.S. soldiers for Afghan children. Fill each resealable plastic bag with the following: one 8×10-inch spiral notebook, one pen, two pencils, a sharpener, a small toy, and a box of raisins. (Because soldiers rotate frequently, please check www.DoOneNiceThing.com for the most current address.)

A few weeks before Christmas 2007, Maj. Walter Woodring sent an e-mail from Afghanistan. He was requesting gifts and donations, but not for himself or his soldiers. He wanted school supplies for Afghan children.

Maj. Woodring wrote: "These kids have absolutely nothing, and when we give them a notebook or pencil, that is the only school item they have. It was 38 degrees, and the kids were taking their exams outside without complaint." Could Americans at home help?

As Do One Nice Thing spread his request, an immediate outpouring of help came from thousands

Do One Nice Thing

of Americans—including middle school sports teams, scout troops, sororities, businesses, Red Hat Society ladies, churches, synagogues, veterans, California Highway Patrol volunteers, Rotary Clubs, and many schools and families. They assembled kits containing 8×10-inch spiral notebooks, a pen, two pencils, a toy, and a treat and put them into individual resealable plastic bags.

After Maj. Woodring completed his tour of duty, Maj. Sean Gustafson and Capt. Ray Gilmore continued to deliver more than 100,000 pounds of school supplies from home to schools around Afghanistan.

••••••••••••••••••••••••

"Thank you tremendously for your support. What we're doing is restoring hope and enabling folks to believe in themselves and their future again. You all back home have got to know that we still have hope here, and it's growing every day."—Maj. Sean Gustafson

> **Another idea: Donate to Operation Dreamseed (www.OperationDreamseed.org). Funds buy school supplies for needy kids in Afghanistan. The organization was founded by Maj. Todd Schmidt when he was deployed there.**

Debbie Tenzer

We've Got You Covered

Donate a blanket for an Iraqi or Afghan family by visiting www.blankets.com and clicking on Donations, Soldiers Helping Those in Need.

A blanket is a source of warmth, comfort, and security as every child knows. But what if we had no blankets? A selfless combat medic serving in northern Iraq thought about that. Sgt. Steve Stephens from Oregon saw many families suffer through a cold Iraqi winter without heat, electricity, or blankets.

"There are a large number of displaced Iraqis living in Mosul and the surrounding areas who don't have a lot and could use a blanket or two," said Stephens. So he decided to get them some blankets.

With the help of six of his fellow soldiers in the First Cavalry Division, he launched Soldiers Helping Those In Need—Iraq. Monica Barbuscia at Blankets .com in Seattle made it possible by agreeing to sell blankets online without any profit. All a donor needed to do was spend a few dollars and a few minutes at a computer, and a blanket would be sent from the U.S.

Do One Nice Thing

to Iraq. Thousands of blankets were sent, and Sgt. Stephens reported what happened when his convoy made the first delivery:

"We had just five minutes to set up security, and then we went to work unloading the truck. People were already starting to come up the hillside. They had come from the outskirts of Al Kush to get a blanket. They own little, at most; their homes had been destroyed by insurgents.

"One recipient told me that he was starting to form a democratic council for his people, and asked if the Army had bought the blankets for them. I smiled and told him, 'No, sir. The blankets came from the kind people of America.' Suddenly he hugged me and shook my hand. As he walked away he said, 'Please tell them thank you.'

"After three hours we were ready to head back. A man stopped me before we could throw the empty blanket boxes back in the truck. He asked if he could have the boxes. I said "Yes," however curiosity got the best of me and I had to ask why. He said they could burn the cardboard to make fires for baking bread. Imagine, they even used the boxes! There was nothing to take back to base with us except the memories. I just wish the media could have been there so

Debbie Tenzer

that people back home could have seen the softer
side of war."

• •

"I joined Sgt. Stephens's committee because I have
been out in the cities of Iraq and I have seen the devastation that has occurred. And yet the Iraqi people
still have hope. I would like to show them that they are
not the only ones who have hope. So do I. And if I can
do something to help them, I will."—PFC Sandi Brown

Do One Nice Thing

Operation Paperback

Have you read any good books lately? Would a deployed soldier enjoy them? Send paperbacks to deployed military personnel through Operation Paperback (www.OperationPaperback.org).

Service members are eager for new reading material, and it's also a wonderful way to recycle your books. The organization provides names and addresses of service members to whom you can send your books.

"I have made several shipments; the largest was about twenty-five books. I have collected books at work too. One person gave up her entire collection of Harry Potter books for me to send. Even though it's called Operation Paperback, I have sent a number of hardcovers, which is fine. I get thank-you notes from the recipients as well as from their families back home. That's just the icing on the cake."
—Ellen

Debbie Tenzer

You can also purchase new books online at www
.BooksAMillion.com. Click on Books, then Books for
Troops. The company will address and send the
books directly to deployed service members.

Do One Nice Thing

The Magic Words

Thank a service member.

*Send an e-mail to thank a service member at www
.LetsSayThanks.com or donate a phone card so service
members can call home: Buy cards through AAFES—the
Army and Air Force Exchange Service (www.aafes.com).
You can also send gifts to service members through
www.anysoldier.com.*

Some people in New Hampshire express their
thanks in person at the Pease Air Terminal in Portsmouth. Military flights land there for refueling before
leaving the United States, or when they return from
overseas. The Pease Greeters, as they are known, are
the first people to welcome service members home to
American soil, or the last people to give them a hug
before they leave.

························

"The troops are generally not aware that there will be
between fifty and a hundred-plus people to greet
them when they land at the airport, and they are absolutely overwhelmed. When they step through the
doors, the cheering, hugging, and crying starts.

"The last plane I helped greet had about 130 or so
troops on it. It takes a while for them to get through

Debbie Tenzer

the crowds of greeters who line the aisles. They hug back and their smiles are a real gift.

"Coffee, doughnuts, and various treats are provided. The troops are usually in Portsmouth, depending on the weather, for one to one and a half hours before they get back on the plane and head to their home base.

"A company in Portsmouth has donated a bank of phones for them to use free of charge to call anywhere in the country to say 'I'm home!,' or a last good-bye before they leave the country. Most of us have our cell phones at the ready as well, so no one misses out on making a call when time is short.

"My first time at the airport was at 3:00 a.m. I got back home about 5:30, slept for an hour, and went to work. Each time I feel like it really is a gift to me from our service members—a wonderful chance to give back to those who put themselves in harm's way, one flight at a time."—Ellen

Do One Nice Thing

Uncle Sam
Wants Who?

James Bond, Pirates of the Caribbean, Rambo, The Wizard of Oz . . .

> **Send new DVDs, CDs, and other gifts to deployed U.S. service members. Also letters of support from you will be treasured. Mail to Operation Gratitude, Carolyn Blashek, 16444 Refugio Road, Encino, CA 91436.**

Carolyn Blashek tried to enlist in the military but they turned her down: They told her she was too old. So the lawyer-turned-stay-at-home mom invented her own way to support the fight against terrorism. She founded Operation Gratitude to send care packages and letters of support to troops deployed overseas.

It started in her suburban living room in 2003, one package at a time. Now Operation Gratitude has sent more than 400,000 packages to individual service members. Carolyn said, "Our mission has always been twofold: first, to lift morale and put a smile on a service member's face, and second to provide an av-

Debbie Tenzer

enue for all Americans to express their appreciation to our military."

Boxes are packed lovingly by volunteers, and contain gifts donated by grateful individuals as well as by companies. Each package includes snacks, entertainment items, personal-care products, and a warm, personal message. There's also an occasional "wowwee!" surprise. SPC Michael "Shaun" Gallagher was delighted when he received a package of gifts during his deployment in Iraq. But when he ripped open an envelope in the box and discovered the keys to a brand-new Jeep Liberty, his day was even better!

When the newly promoted Cpl. Gallagher returned home six months later, he received not only the Jeep but a second surprise as well. He had planned to have a tribute painted on the Jeep's hood with the names of his unit's fallen soldiers. But with some input from his family, Operation Gratitude and Chrysler had the memorial painted while he was still in Iraq. They presented it to him during an emotional ceremony at Fort Lewis, Washington, when the unit came home.

. . . .

"I am deeply touched and gratified every time I receive an e-mail, letter, or picture from the troops telling us that our packages made a difference to them. And I am

Do One Nice Thing

very proud when I look at our thousands of volunteers and supporters, who hail from every part of the country, every race, religion, socioeconomic background, and every point on the political spectrum, and I see them working together in pursuit of a common cause: to say thank-you to the men and women defending our nation."—Carolyn

Our Military Kids

Help children of deployed National Guard and Reserve soldiers by making a donation of any amount at www.OurMilitaryKids.org.

Military children don't have it easy. They live with both the stress of family separation and the fact that their parents have dangerous jobs. They're told to "take care" of the at-home parent, while they worry about the parent who is away. No matter their age, they can become depressed and may not know how to express their feelings.

Some help is available on or near military bases. But more than 70,000 children don't live on bases and can't access their services. These are the children of National Guard and Army Reserve soldiers. Before September 11, 2001, most National Guard soldiers had nonmilitary careers, serving one weekend per month and two weeks in the summer. But since 9/11, they have been sent on repeated long deployments to Iraq and Afghanistan. Many families—especially the at-home parents—face severe financial and emotional strain.

Worried children often lose focus in school and

Do One Nice Thing

need help. Other kids manage their schoolwork well, but would really benefit from after-school sports, music, or art. Often, when the kids need a hobby or tutor most, they can't afford one.

Our Military Kids collects and grants funds to help these children. Every penny goes directly to help the kids (overhead is paid by corporate donations). For example, $25 pays for a month of martial arts classes; $35, a month of ballet and tap lessons; $50, a weekly tutoring session; $100, the fee for football season. With tutoring in particular, the impact can be fast and dramatic. When the kids receive a little extra attention and understanding, their confidence and grades shoot up.

"Words simply cannot express my great appreciation. Keeping my daughter busy and on the most normal schedule I can is the best way I have to help her deal with the sadness and worry she feels. I write this hoping you truly know what your work does for these military kids, what a difference you are making, and how much we as families deeply appreciate your efforts."—a grateful mother

Debbie Tenzer

A Taste of Home

Invite a service member to a holiday or weekend meal in your home.

Al was a soldier serving in South Korea, when he was invited to dinner by Ruth and Ed, an American couple temporarily living there. "When Ruth and Ed invited me to dinner—wow! Hours of preparation were evident. To me the dining room table looked like a hotel buffet. It was filled with platters of beautiful food, but the food was secondary to the family's warmth. These many years later I am still personally grateful for the friendship and hospitality they showed me while I was a soldier overseas. They made me feel at home and part of a family."

A few years later when they had all returned to the States, Ruth and Ed invited Al home for dinner again, and he was introduced to their niece, Sue. Apparently Al was intrigued by more than the food: This year Al and Sue are celebrating their twenty-fifth wedding anniversary.

Do One Nice Thing

The Best Medicine

Donate some of your airline miles so family members can visit a wounded service member in the hospital: visit www.FisherHouse.org and click on Hero Miles.

A casualty assistance officer calls, and suddenly somewhere in America a military family's nightmare begins: Their loved one has been wounded.

At that moment for a mom, dad, husband, or wife, the mind goes blank. Just minutes before, he or she was managing an office, teaching a class, or chatting with a neighbor. A young mother might have been nursing a baby. Then normal life slams to a halt.

How did it happen? How can I get there? Where will I stay? How will I pay for it?

Thankfully, no family has to face those questions alone. When the family is called, a casualty officer also notifies the nonprofit Fisher House Foundation in Maryland. The Fisher House motto is "A family's love is good medicine," and their team snaps into action. Fisher House personnel obtain all relevant information, call the family, and arrange free transportation to rush them to their wounded loved one's bedside fast.

Debbie Tenzer

This is possible because the foundation administers the Hero Miles airline ticket program. Individuals donate frequent flyer miles to the program, and the Fisher House Foundation pays the security fees—$5 per ticket—from donations. Thousands of free tickets have been provided so far.

That's not all: When a family arrives at the hospital, they can stay at a Fisher House guest house nearby, also free of charge.

· ·

"Having my wife and daughter here is the best inspiration I could ever have. I know I have lots of people in my corner."—Staff Sgt. Justin Shellhammer

Do One Nice Thing

State-of-the-Art
Moral Support

**Send a gas or gift card to wounded
service members and their
families at the Warrior and Family
Support Center (WFSC),
2010 Stanley Road, Suite 95,
Fort Sam Houston, TX 78234.**

Gas cards are especially appreciated because many
families drive two hours each way from Fort Hood to
visit their loved ones in the hospital.

**You can also make an online
donation to the Intrepid
Fallen Heroes Fund
(www.FallenHeroesFund.org)
to assist wounded service
members and their families.**

Brooke Army Medical Center at Fort Sam Houston,
Texas, has a state-of-the-art rehabilitation facility and
the sole military burn unit in the United States. It's a
busy place. Wounded service members have suffered

Debbie Tenzer

extremely serious injuries: burns, loss of limbs, as well as head wounds and internal injuries, requiring hospital treatment for many months—sometimes a year or longer.

Spending time with family accelerates a soldier's recovery, and it's also important for the family. So physicians initiated the Warrior and Family Support Center, the first of its kind. Instead of a sterile hospital environment, it feels like a home with a television, activities, home-baked cookies, and caring people surrounding patients. There are field trips to restaurants, as well as rodeos and ball games.

Judith Markelz is the Center's "Mom," a dynamo manager, as well as a warm, energetic presence watching over everyone. She is 100 percent focused on one thing: doing whatever it takes to help wounded service members—and their families—heal. When they don't know how to solve a problem, whether it is related to scheduling appointments, keeping children occupied, or finding accommodations for visiting family members, Judith and her staff find a way.

....

"I do not know how I would have survived here for nine months without the center. Without them, I have no idea what I would have done by now."—Anonymous

Do One Nice Thing

"I have the best job in the whole world. I get to work with the finest, strongest young men and women in this nation—and the finest families too. It's a privilege."—Judith

From Sea
to Shining Sea

**Send encouragement to an ill or
wounded service member by
mailing a picture postcard from
your state. Write a "we-are-with-
you message," then put your card in
an envelope and mail it to 21st TSC,
Medical Transient Detachment,
ATTN: Soldiers' Angels, UNIT 23203,
APO AE 09263.**

Hundreds of ill or wounded American service members arrive every month at Landstuhl Regional Medical Center in Germany, usually in the same dirty
uniforms they were wearing when they were evacu-
ated. And it is often weeks before their belongings
reach them. To help in the meantime, there's Soldiers'
Angels.

The organization was founded by Patti Patton-
Bader, a mother of two soldiers. (She's the niece of
World War II legend Gen. George Patton.) When her
older son was deployed in 2003, he told her that some
soldiers in his unit did not receive any mail from
home. Patti quickly contacted a few friends and family

Do One Nice Thing

members and asked if they would each support a soldier. Within a short time, Soldiers' Angels went from a mom shipping a few extra care packages to an Internet community with hundreds of thousands of volunteer Angels worldwide sending support to the deployed, their relatives at home, veterans, and families of the fallen.

Soldiers' Angels also provides "welcome kits" for hospitalized service members. Each kit contains travel-size hygiene products, an international calling card, a sweatshirt, and a handmade blanket. Now it can also contain a picture of home sent with love from you.

••••••••••••••••••••••••

"You can even design your own postcard with your family standing in front of some cool place you visited. There are so many places in America that are fascinating, and if just one soldier felt America was there with him or her, it would be worth it."—Sandy

Debbie Tenzer

Sew Much Comfort

Send a new package of boxer or basketball shorts—size L or XL—to Sew Much Comfort Distribution Center, 3170 Rodenbeck Drive, Beavercreek, OH 45432. If you would like to volunteer your sewing skills, information is available at www.SewMuchComfort.org.

Hospital gowns are *so drafty.* Unfortunately they are often the only clothing option for thousands of wounded service members. They endure years of prosthetic fittings, surgeries, and rehabilitation, and regular clothing doesn't fit over their braces and casts.

Now there's a better choice, thanks to Sew Much Comfort. The organization's volunteer seamstresses across the United States sew Velcro into the seams of new shorts, pants, and shirts. The organization has provided tens of thousands of adapted garments to more than a hundred military hospitals for free.

Wounded service members can "rip" open the garments at the Velcroed seams, slide in, and then press the seams shut. The Sew Much Comfort clothes are not only more comfortable and dignified to wear,

Do One Nice Thing

they are a symbol of normalcy—normal clothes for resuming a normal life, as opposed to a hospital gown for someone who is ailing. Thanks to Sew Much Comfort, wounded heroes can get up every morning and do what the rest of us take for granted: put on some clothes and go out.

....

"On behalf of the troops of Task Force Freedom in Northern Iraq, I want to sincerely thank you for putting your heart, hands, and ingenuity together to help the wounded. Your organization has put forth remarkable efforts to restore pride and dignity to injured military personnel and civilians. Your specialized clothing brings much more than warmth to the injured person; it also is an immeasurable step in healing the mind as well."—Maj. Gen. David M. Rodriguez

Debbie Tenzer

Give an Hour

Are you a mental health professional? Donate your services for an hour to help combat veterans and their families. Visit www.GiveanHour.org if you, a friend, or a family member is a combat veteran and needs help.

The Global War on Terror is a war like no other. In past wars, the enemy wore a uniform. Armies knew where battle lines were, and soldiers fought each other. Not now. In Iraq and Afghanistan terrorists target civilians, and an encounter with an innocent-looking man, woman, or even child can be deadly. It's hard to know who the enemy is, and that along with the other revulsions of combat are agonizing for our soldiers.

The number of post-traumatic stress injuries our combat veterans have sustained is high, and multiple deployments have pounded soldiers (and their loved ones) with enormous pressure. If they had injured an arm or a leg, they'd seek help. But because their pain is psychological, they hesitate. The Department of Defense is working hard to encourage soldiers to seek

Do One Nice Thing

help. Psychological screenings and follow-up appointments are mandatory. But many returning veterans don't reveal their symptoms because they don't want to be branded with a "mental" stigma. So where else can vets go?

Give an Hour is not part of the military. It is a nonprofit organization that offers mental health care to veterans and their families, as well as unmarried partners. And it's free. Give an Hour professionals believe that most returning veterans would not need mental health care if not for the extreme circumstances of their military service. Even the bravest among us can feel chained by fear, and there is no shame in that. Counseling can help them break free and move forward with their lives.

· ·

"Listen with the ear of your heart."—St. Benedict

Debbie Tenzer

In Honor of Veterans

Show your appreciation for veterans by helping out at the Veterans Administration:

→ Donate tickets to a ball game, zoo, museum, or other local attraction.

→ Help a vet fill out a benefit claim form.

→ Push a library cart in a VA hospital or long-term-care facility.

→ Mail a pack of playing cards or a board game.

→ Go to: www.volunteer.va.gov and click on Volunteer or Donate.

Do One Nice Thing

The Song That Doesn't End

**Make a donation, volunteer at
a USO hospitality center,
or encourage your company
to become a USO supporter
(www.uso.org/howtohelp).**

Mallory Lewis, entertainer and Emmy-winning producer of her late mother Shari's television shows, is a goodwill ambassador of the USO. Like her mother, Mallory is also a gifted ventriloquist and puppeteer. After Shari Lewis's death in 1998, family friend Dom DeLuise advised Mallory to keep puppet Lamb Chop alive. So Mallory began performing with Lamb Chop. At her own expense, she and Lamb Chop entertain military families all over the world.

"Lambie and I performed at a welcome-home celebration at Fort Hood for soldiers returning from Iraq and their families. When I was waiting backstage, a general approached me and told me about an incident just before his soldiers 'took Baghdad.'

"The soldiers had been tense—it was the moment they'd been waiting for. One soldier spontaneously started singing into his headset 'The Song

Debbie Tenzer

That Doesn't End.'* It's the song that is associated with Mom because it was the theme song for her TV show, *Lamb Chop's Play-Along."*

> *It is the song that doesn't end*
> *It just goes on and on, my friends*
> *Some people started singing it, not knowing*
> *   what it was,*
> *And they'll continue singing it forever just*
> *   because,*
> *It is the song that doesn't end.*

"After the first soldier started singing, more and more soldiers joined in. It united them, lifted them up, and reminded them of home."

That night when Mallory came on stage, the audience—fifty thousand soldiers and family members—astonished her by bursting into "The Song That Doesn't End." Their roaring voices charged through the skies and surely reached Shari in Heaven. Mallory stood on stage with Lamb Chop for what seemed like a very long time looking out at all the brave young faces, and the families, and even Lamb Chop was speechless.

Do One Nice Thing

8

·······

Just Click!
Do One Nice Thing
Online

This chapter gathers together all of the nice things threaded throughout the book that are just a click away. I created it for the harried and busy among us, which seems to be everybody these days.

Do One Nice Thing with Friends and Family

Donate to charity when you shop on eBay. Look for the charity ribbons or search for charities. If you're a seller, list items to benefit a cause that you care about. Visit www.eBayGivingWorks.com.

Do One Nice Thing for Children

Help a school through Donors Choose, where teachers post requests online for books, supplies, technology, and more. Then you can select the way you'd like to help at www.DonorsChoose.org.

Do One Nice Thing for Pets and the Planet

→ "Adopt" an endangered animal through the World Wildlife Fund at www.WorldWildlife.org.

→ Purchase pet toys and treats online for Best Friends Animal Society and Sanctuary at www.BestFriends.org.

→ Help Abandoned Animals: Just click www.TheAnimalRescueSite.com to donate free food to them.

→ Help emergency responders and their dogs by supporting the Search Dog Foundation at www.Searchdogfoundation.org.

→ Help preserve rain forests around the world by clicking on www.TheRainforestSite.com.

→ Donate free food to abandoned animals: Play the Bow Wow Dog Trivia game at

Debbie Tenzer

www.FreeKibble.com and Meow Cat Trivia game at www.FreeKibbleKat.com.

→ Reduce junk mail. Delete your name and address from some of the senders' mailing lists. It's easy to do on the Direct Marketing Association website: https://www.dmachoice.org.

→ Swap goods with other recyclers on www.freecycle.org.

Do One Nice Thing That Heals

→ Sign up online to be an organ and tissue donor at www.DonateLife.net/.

→ To support breast cancer research at the City of Hope, contribute to Jump for the Cause at www.JumpfortheCause.com.

→ Join the online support group of breast cancer survivors, friends, and family at www.Pink-Link.org.

→ Donate a free mammogram for a woman who cannot afford one at www.TheBreastCancerSite.com.

→ Donate vitamins and nourishing food for children, homeless, and the elderly at www.NourishAmerica.org.

Do One Nice Thing

Do One Nice Thing in Town

Individuals and food companies can find out how to donate food to a food bank or make a donation so food can reach a food bank at www.FeedingAmerica.org.

Do One Nice Thing
Around the Globe

→ Support your favorite charity or school whenever you search and shop on the Internet at www.GoodSearch.com and www.GoodShop.com.

→ Play the Free Rice game at www.FreeRice.com. For every word you get right, advertisers donate rice to the United Nations World Food Program to feed hungry people in developing countries.

→ Click www.TheHungerSite.com daily to donate free food to starving people.

→ Help end hunger by donating money to Heifer International or Feeding America at www.heifer.org or www.FeedingAmerica.org.

→ Make a "micro-loan" of $25 or more through Kiva at www.Kiva.org.

Debbie Tenzer

➜ Donate a goat in Rwanda for $30 or participate in other Bears Without Borders projects at www.BearsWithoutBorders.org.

➜ Donate $30 to buy solar cookers for a Darfur family at www.JewishWorldwatch.org/ RefugeeRelief.

Do One Nice Thing

Do One Nice Thing for Soldiers

→ Donate to Operation Dreamseed to help educate children in Afghanistan at www.OperationDreamseed.org.

→ Make a donation of any amount at www.OurMilitaryKids.org.

→ Send an e-mail to thank a service member at www.LetsSayThanks.com.

→ Donate a phone card so a soldier can call home at www.aafes.com.

→ Buy and send books to deployed service members at www.BooksAMillion.com; click on Books, then Books for Troops.

→ "Adopt" a soldier at www.anysoldier.com and www.soldiersangels.com.

→ Donate some of your airline miles at www.FisherHouse.org. Click on Hero Miles.

→ Make a donation to the Intrepid Fallen Heroes Fund at www.FallenHeroesFund.org to assist wounded service members and their families.

→ Make a donation to the USO at www.uso.org/howtohelp.

Debbie Tenzer

The Power of Half a Sandwich

A nice thing might not seem like much because it's easy to do. Its impact, though, is often surprisingly profound:

→ Lt. Col. Tim Maxwell, a Marine, sustained a traumatic brain injury in Iraq but he's not complaining. He's helping other wounded Marines recover at the Wounded Warrior Barracks at Camp Lejeune, North Carolina. I thanked him for his service to our country and asked if we could help him. He replied, "Wow! Just 'thank you' is great— really superb. I appreciate it." Within days Do One Nice Thing members sent hundreds of e-mails to him to say "thank you." He answered,

"Debbie, I have received *tons* of e-mails. We print them out and hang them all over the walls. There are so many! Thank *you.*"

➜ Jet Blue pilot John Hicks's Long Beach–Washington, D.C., flight was about to take off, when he made an announcement. Because of work, he was missing his twin sons' fifteenth birthday, but he had an idea. Would the passengers help him spring a little birthday surprise on his boys? Sure! He called them on his cell phone, and 144 passengers and crew sang "Happy Birthday" to his children. The boys were flabbergasted, their dad was delighted, and the passengers enjoyed themselves too.

➜ AnnMarie often orders a sandwich for lunch in a Manhattan restaurant. She eats half and asks the waiter to wrap up the other half. When she leaves, she gives it to a homeless person on the street. How many of us think twice about half a sandwich? But if you're starving, or your child is, half a sandwich can save a life and restore your faith in humanity.

What is "half a sandwich" in your life? What are the things you can do to make someone else's life better? This book offers many suggestions, but other fantastic ideas aren't in the book. You will create

Debbie Tenzer

them yourself. I invite you to share them with Nice-o-holics around the world by contacting me at DoOneNiceThing.com.

Remember this: When you help someone, you give them hope. And the more hope you give, the more hopeful *you* feel.

Are you hooked yet?

Now you know what to do, and you know when to do it. It's so simple! Just do a nice thing for someone every week. Use the journal on the following pages to keep track of the nice things you do in the coming year.

The world is full of good people making a difference every week. You can be one of them. Become a Nice-o-holic and join us every Monday to do one nice thing.

After we fix Mondays, we'll tackle Tuesdays.

Do One Nice Thing

Do One Nice Thing Journal

The end of this book is really a beginning—a beginning of your recorded legacy of kind deeds. The following pages are your Nice Journal for you to write down the nice things you do and the dates that you do them. There are fifty-two spaces—one for each Monday of the year.

1. _____
   _____
2. _____
   _____
3. _____
   _____
4. _____
   _____
5. _____
   _____
6. _____
   _____
7. _____
   _____

8. _____
_____
9. _____
_____
10. _____
_____
11. _____
_____
12. _____
_____
13. _____
_____
14. _____
_____
15. _____
_____
16. _____
_____
17. _____
_____
18. _____
_____
19. _____
_____
20. _____
_____

21. _____

22. _____

23. _____

24. _____

25. _____

26. _____

27. _____

28. _____

29. _____

30. _____

31. _____

32. _____

33. _____

34. _____
_____

35. _____
_____

36. _____
_____

37. _____
_____

38. _____
_____

39. _____
_____

40. _____
_____

41. _____
_____

42. _____
_____

43. _____
_____

44. _____
_____

45. _____
_____

46. _____
_____

47. _____

_____

48. _____

_____

49. _____

_____

50. _____

_____

51. _____

_____

52. _____

_____

Join Us

WARNING: Doing one nice thing can be habit-forming. Proceed at your own risk!

Are Mondays tough?

They sure are. Feel better by doing at least one nice thing for someone every Monday to start the new week right. You might feel *so good* that you'll become a Nice-o-holic.

Join us for more ideas and stories, and to connect with other nice people. We also want to hear about the nice things you're doing. To get nice news delivered, sign up for our e-mails. That's good news in your in-box, free.

We embrace everyone. Working together, it's amazing what we can achieve.

For more information on the many projects and organizations mentioned in this book, please visit www.DoOneNiceThing.com.

You may also write to us at: Do One Nice Thing, 149 South Barrington Avenue, Los Angeles, CA 90049-3310.

Appreciation

I am grateful to:

My terrific team

Scott Mora, the Do One Nice Thing website's intrepid producer and his mighty band at www.tm5150.com, and John Michael Pugsley, our award-winning creative director, who has also designed for Disney, Starbucks, and Coca-Cola. John and Scott joined me even though I could barely pay them, and they're with me still. They solve every problem with imagination, patience, and humor, and there would be no Do One Nice Thing without them. (Scott's online studio is www.5150.com and John's is www.jmpdesign.com.)

Bonnie Solow, my spectacular literary agent and book-birthing coach, was my friend for many years before she became my agent. Always looking for ways to help others, she contributed ideas to the Do One Nice Thing website before I ever thought of writing a book. Her vision and heart infuse every page.

Crown Publishing: Executive Editor Heather Jackson swept me off my feet during our very first conversation. She is smart, funny, and compassionate, and focuses like a laser without losing sight of the big picture. This book has zillions of details and Heather deserves full credit for organizing them in the most reader-friendly way.

When I chose Heather I had no idea that all my Crown "in-laws" would be fabulous too, but they are: publishers Tina Constable and Philip Patrick, and the whole Crown team—Patty Berg, Amy Boorstein, Alisha Cantrell, Lauren Dong, Jill Flaxman, Nupoor Gordon, Linda Kaplan, Heather Proulx, Annsley Rosner, Karin Schulze, Siri Silleck, Penny Simon, Nicole Sprinkle, and Jie Yang.

Annabelle Stevens is known as one of Hollywood's top publicists, and fortunately she agreed to be my publicist too. She is an expert on the entertainment business (her clients included the late Paul Newman), but her real passion is philanthropy. She is energetic, wise, and kind, and a joy to work with, www.annabellestevens.com.

Kristin Loberg, my delightful editorial advisor, did a very nice thing. She donated part of her editing fee to Net Results Junior Tennis to give a boost to underprivileged athletic kids in Denver.

The Do One Nice Thing Board of Advisors: My longtime pals, Jonathan Schreiber, Christine Hyland, and Wendi Knox extended themselves far beyond the call of friendship. Luckily for me, they also happen to be savvy communications professionals.

Jonathan is a marketing strategist who is an expert in the nonprofit sector. He has created campaigns for international fund-raising organizations, medical centers, schools, and more. He is also my go-to guy for out-of-the-box ideas. Brilliant.

Chris is a national development expert and trainer who finds funding, housing, schools, and health care for the poor, and she does it while practicing St. Benedict's message, "Listen with the ear of your heart." (I like the quote so much that I included it in Chapter 7.) Chris contributed numerous imaginative ideas for this book.

Wendi, who has won every possible advertising award, touches women with her own brand of wit and wisdom, Oh My Goddess, www.OhMyGoddess.com. She graciously read and commented on every incarnation of this book, and when I occasionally felt overwhelmed she reminded me that the difference between "imperfect" and "I'm perfect" is just an apostrophe.

U.S. Service Members I cherish:

Have you ever tried to thank a service member? In my experience they always reply, "Thank *you,* ma'am." That's how they are—selfless. I'll try to thank them anyway. Many service members in Afghanistan, Iraq, Kuwait, Kosovo, and Germany generously took time to correspond with me and described to me what their lives are like. I am particularly grateful to Lt. Col. Anthony Boyda, Capt. Ray Gilmore, Maj. Sean Gustafson, Col. Mitchell Marovitz (Ret.), and Lt. Col. Walter Woodring for their guidance, optimism, and kindness, as well as their often-hilarious e-mails.

Spectacular friends I'm grateful for:

Lenore Bruckner, Alan and Dana Edelstein, Rona Edwards, Barbara Eskowitz, Karin Mueller Frank, Frank Garner, Israel Grinberg, Sarah Johannessen, Scott Landsbaum, Sue Leavitt, Charles Marcus, Jean Oh, the Palti family, Ziva Paltiziano, Bob Pollack, Ricardo Tellez, and Rabbi Morley Feinstein.

Tamar "Ace" Raff, my college roommate and longtime buddy, has shared adventures with me on three continents, including climbing Mt. Sinai at 4 a.m. Her love for children is boundless, and she has dedicated her life to teaching them how to make the world better.

Brad "Martini" Chambers is a beloved Los Angeles radio host, producer, and Rat Pack music expert. He's got the world on a string and gave me a home on his radio show every Monday. He has also helped countless artists rise in the music business, www.MartiniInTheMorning.com.

Vitka Kovner is living proof that even when you've lost everything, helping someone can restore your hope. As a teenage partisan in Europe, she fought the Nazis. Later she became a psychologist in Israel and pioneered a unique art therapy for children. Once when missiles rained down near her kibbutz, I asked her if she was worried. She replied, "No." Why not, Vitka? "Because worrying does not help."

Tamar Gale is my friend, teacher, and inspiration: Whenever I ask her how she is, she proclaims, "Excellent!" Is everything excellent? No, but some things are, and that's how she reminds herself to be consciously thankful every day.

Rhonda Gale (no relation to Tamar, except that I love them both) was the first friend I confided the idea of Do One Nice Thing to. If you look up "enthusiasm" in the dictionary, her picture is there (or should be). She is also an astute entertainment attorney, Nice-o-holic, and connector par excellence. Time and again she spread the word about Do One Nice Thing projects to all her friends, and Radiant Rhonda has *many* friends.

The greatest blessings in my life— my family:

Tenzers: Albert, Isobel, Jamee, Michael, Josh, Maddy, Lily, Moira, and Stuart.

Grosses: Felice; Rebecca; my brother, Bill, whose

memory blesses me; my sweet sister, Karyn (whose story is in Chapter 5); and especially my role models, Mom and Dad—Jackie and Sylvan. They've spent their whole lives quietly helping others.

My children, Daniel, Ben, and Rachel, who are the light of my life.

And most of all David, who makes me laugh every day and loves me even when I'm skating on thin nice.